Plotted

A Literary Atlas

By Andrew DeGraff

For my favorite teacher, my mom. —**AD**

AN IMPRINT OF
ZEST BOOKS

35 Stillman Street, Suite 121, San Francisco, CA 94107 | www.zestbooks.net
Connect with Zest! zestbooks.net/blog | zestbooks.net/contests | twitter.com/zestbooks | facebook.com/BooksWithATwist

Manufactured in the U.S.A. | 4500552494 | DOW 10 9 8 7 6 5 4 3 2 1

Plotted

A Literary Atlas

By Andrew DeGraff

With essays by Daniel Harmon

Table of Contents

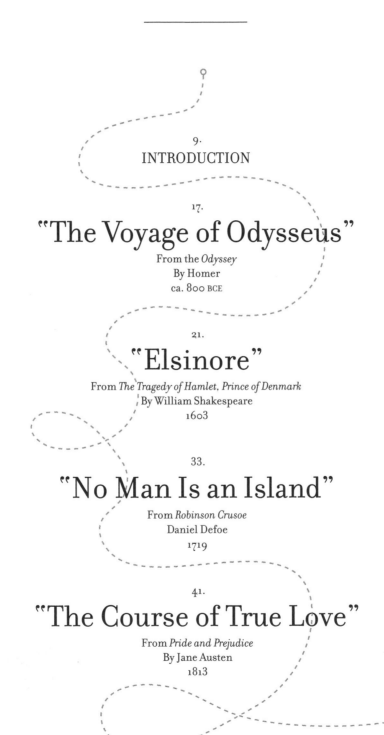

Introduction

By Andrew DeGraff

2015

It's hard to say where *Plotted* came from, exactly, but if I had to point to a single person, I think I'd have to go with my mom. She's a teacher — a really good one — and she's always stressed the importance of context. "You need to understand the big picture in order to see what you still have to learn..." "You need to know how things fit together before you'll be able to take them apart." Context, in her view, is essential for understanding complex things. And I think I agree with her on that. These maps vary pretty widely when it comes to what they show and how they show it, but they all resulted from my desire to provide a spatial context for some of my favorite literary landscapes. I wanted to paint what I imagined (or rather, what great authors allowed me to imagine).

I first started doing these kinds of maps for movies, not books. I did maps for *Star Wars*, *Indiana Jones*, *The Shining*, and *The Lord of the Rings*. Most of the creative work in those cases was focused on providing an integrated experience of the given landscape rather than deciding what the Overlook Hotel or Mordor looked like. I wanted to return to those places, not revise them. But a somewhat unanticipated benefit from those mapmaking exercises is that I was forced to expand upon what the movies provided. I needed to plot continuous journeys for characters who, on film, only exist in discrete episodes. The dots had to be connected, but before that could be done, the blank spaces had to be filled in. And when the maps were completed, I felt like the places had become a little bit more real.

I hadn't necessarily planned on mapping books, though. In fact, I was thinking about taking a break from maps altogether when Daniel Harmon (this book's editor and essayist) first approached me about doing something mappy and bookish. As the son of a teacher, I've always been a pretty big reader, and my soundtrack of choice while painting is usually an audiobook rather than an album, so the possibility of tackling classic works that didn't yet have a definitive visual representation was uniquely appealing. And that ended up being the first restriction that we settled on: we didn't want to do books that had already been mapped. (So *The Hobbit* was out; as was *The Chronicles of Narnia*; as was *A Song of Ice and Fire*.) We also wanted to avoid creating maps for books that already had a definitive visual representation — a movie or TV show or even a cover that seemed to have settled what the book "looked like." (So no *Peter Pan*; no *Rebecca*; no *Harry Potter*.) I wanted to start from scratch — scratch in this case being the stories themselves — as much as I possibly could.

Because each of these maps requires a pretty intense amount of time and labor — both for the research and for the actual drafting and painting — we had to restrict our final number of books and stories to the nineteen that you see here, which meant a lot of cuts to our initial list of fifty works (an insane number, in retrospect). Maintaining diversity across genres, centuries, and authors was also very important to me, as was including my own personal favorites, regardless of their overall appeal. (I'm still a little devastated that *Dune* didn't make the final cut.) But with just nineteen works stretching from the ninth century BCE to 1973, there are going to be a lot of gaps. Anyway, suffice it to say that we have plenty of ideas for expansions and sequels.

So that's the rough process by which we selected the books and stories that you see represented here. But that still leaves the question of why the chosen books were mapped the way they were. And the short answer is that I tried to let the books guide the maps. Daniel and I would have long conversations about each map before I began my first draft, but those conversations were usually more about literature than they were about cartography or design. In some cases, as with *Moby Dick* and *Hamlet*, there was no shortage of possible interpretations, and as a result we wanted to find a way to try out something new. (*Moby Dick* is also one of the few works for which a fairly definitive map already exists — "The Voyage of the Pequod," by artist Everett Henry.) In other cases, as with *Around the World in Eighty Days* and *Watership Down*, we had no grander idea than simply to plot the characters' journeys — and that left simply the question of aesthetics. But for the remainder, the central question really was, "What is this book about?" I won't pretend that we've answered those questions, but they were central to the design process. (They were also half the fun of doing this book.) Which brings me back to the question of context.

There's been a huge increase recently in infographic/data visualization work for a popular audience. There have also been a number of great books about intelligent design (not that kind) and the history of maps. (Check out the "Further Reading" section at the back of the book for a quick rundown of standouts in the latter category.) For the maps in *Plotted*, I tried to operate in a kind of middle ground between infographic work and cartography. I tend to think of both as fairly two-dimensional; and without the added dimension of depth (to say nothing of time), it's impossible to provide that sense of "diving in."

However, before moving on I have to address the things that have been left out in the construction of these maps. And there was a lot. A two-hour movie of a 300-page novel leaves a lot of the book on the cutting-room floor. A narrative can flow in and out of multiple perspectives in the course of a novel; it can veer from reality to the realm of magic and back again in a paragraph, or it can jump a thousand years in a sentence. So, translating the 400 pages of *Watership Down* into six pages of maps is, for lack of a better word, impossible. But that doesn't mean it's not worth trying.

Perhaps the best way to explain this deficit without excusing it is to say that, for each of these literary works, I attempted to map at least one aspect of the given book as completely as I could. In *Watership Down*, I mapped the physical movements of twenty-two rabbits and one black-headed gull. The characters' journeys (and their various resting places) became the basis for the map. And that makes sense for many of these books. The resulting maps may not offer enough information to understand the plot fully, but neither will reading a single chapter of *Moby Dick* explain the full majesty of that novel. But that one chapter does at least tell you something important. It doesn't say everything, but it certainly says something. Much as the skyline of New York creates a rough map of the bedrock that it rests upon, or in the way that a map of the London Tube can tell you where the population centers are, these maps provide a sense of contour — sometimes literal and sometimes metaphorical — for their literary inspirations. They reveal the focal points of the plot, without delineating every single point contained within in the plot itself.

That being said, this was always going to be a fairly subjective enterprise. My vision of the Pequod will not be everyone's. But I did try to be as objective — and historically accurate — as I could be. This means that Ellison's New York of the 1930s is built out of the city as it existed at that time. The Chrysler Building and the Empire State Building had just been completed, creating a new, taller midtown district. The bridges along the East River were completed in the early 1900s, and many of the buildings downtown are based on real buildings of the time. The Liberty Paints factory, however, is a complete fiction — a Frankenstein construction made up of various factories from that time and a few actual paint factories that I was able to find. There aren't that many though, and most of the ones that were being photographed in the 1930s had been built well prior to the Jazz Age. We can infer from the lack of photos that a paint factory job was not one that people frequently memorialized on the mantle above the fireplace. We can also infer that I basically made up that particular factory from scratch.

What surprised me in my subjectively objective work was the amount of real locations, ships, buildings, and settings that appeared in these largely fictional publications. Jules Verne's tale of circumnavigation is filled with real railroads and mostly real ships. And whenever they were real, I did my best to find them. All of the architecture that appears in *Plotted* is at best a good approximation of regional styles from the given time, and at worst a pretty good guess at the same. For less reality-based stories like "Those Who Walk Away from Omelas" and "Library of Babel" I was left with just the author's words. But that's not a bad place to be either.

"The Library of Babel" does deserve some special mention here, as it is a bit of an outlier in another sense. Borges's story has no real characters (the narrator is just one librarian among many) and no real journey — and so the map lacks the usual character route — but the story does still move. We go from an understanding of the single cell to an understanding of the surrounding cells, to a dawning consciousness of the universe that repeats endlessly around us. And that "us" reveals how central the reader is to the experience of that story. Because the reader is, in a way, the main character — which presents a unique problem: how to include the reader in the map. But the answer to that question is contained above. As a reader of the story and as the mapmaker, I'm already contained within the map. Or rather, just outside it. That perspective should always be visible.

The other outlier is the second spread of Frederick Douglass's *Narrative*. As the only autobiography in *Plotted* (and only work of nonfiction, in fact), it gave rise to a map that owed more to reality but which also diverted substantially from its source. Frederick Douglass was such a monumental figure that we thought it would further illustrate his context in history to show some highlights from his life after his narrative as well. His book was the story of his life, after all, and his life went off in several new directions after the *Narrative* was published. It therefore seemed important to show Douglass's life as well as his life story as it was contained within his original book.

If this project reveals anything to you about me, it should be that I am firmly in the camp that values the journey over the destination. (It should also be said that I am an unrepentant spoiler of plots — so buyer beware.) I think these maps tend to be best viewed by someone who has actually read the books, but that may be because that's the only way I see them. Still, my hope is that they can also entice people who haven't read these books into picking them up. Short of that, I think the maps can serve as visual placeholders for people who haven't yet been introduced to these books. When *Watership Down* is mentioned, you'll know that it's about rabbits in the English countryside, and not about a ship lost at sea. In that way I hope to place some images in your contextual framework, for both the books you've read and the ones you haven't.

This introduction notwithstanding, I tried not to overthink these maps as *maps* before I began sketching them. I tried to remain as true as possible to the works while also offering something that felt new — or at least exciting enough to try. The fact that we had to leave so much out in the transition from words to images was liberating, and I hope the end result will have something to offer to casual readers and devoted bookworms alike. And for readers who may be too young for some of the books in question (as I am too young for "The Lottery" — as everyone is), I hope the maps will serve as an invitation. Like most readers, I know what it is to be seduced by a cover; and like any number of great book covers, the *Plotted* maps are intended to be simultaneously literal and metaphorical. One way or the other, they seek to draw you in.

One last thing about maps. There's no escaping the fact that maps today are used primarily as a means for locating ourselves and our destinations. But those are the kinds of maps that we also discard upon arrival. These maps are different, I hope. These are maps for people who seek to travel beyond the lives and places that they already know (or think they know). The goal here isn't to become found, but only to become more lost.

Like a poorly informed but over-confident urbanite, I seek to help you get more lost.

"The writer is an explorer. Every step is an advance into new land."

— RALPH WALDO EMERSON

The Voyage of Odysseus

From the *Odyssey*
By Homer
ca. 800 BCE

There's no place like home. You can't go home again. Home is where the heart is — and home is also, obviously, a very metaphorical concept. That's as true now as it was in ancient Greece, when Homer was composing his epic poetry. Odysseus is a character who is born at odds with domestic life. Homer describes him in the opening lines as "the wanderer," and that term is both a fate and a calling. His cunning allows him to seek creative solutions to the unique problems that he faces (threatened by six-headed monsters! held captive by a Cyclops! seduced by a witch!), but it also drives him from one adventure to the next. Odysseus's "home," therefore, is just as much the wider Mediterranean as it is the island of Ithaca. Reunion is in Ithaca, that much is true; but Odysseus is at home wherever he goes.

This map — containing spirits below ground, gods above, and monsters in between — shows Odysseus's world as a place that is both recognizable and yet deeply foreign. The landscape remains much the same; these places often truly existed; and yet, this world blends realistic elements with fantasy in a way that gives us pause. Homer's work pushes beyond the world as most people knew it then, and like many early world maps it seems that the human imagination has picked up where human knowledge left off. Distant seas become home to serpents, and foreign lands give rise to monstrous new species of animals. This is a map of the world as it might be, rather than the world as it is. And it's exciting to return to a time when so much was still unknown, when the margins of our maps were so spacious.

But the *Odyssey* hasn't managed to remain vital simply because of its monstrous imaginings (although that didn't hurt). It's also a very human drama: a love story, a tale of familial reconciliation, a revenge mission, and, of course, an epic journey. We get the sense that we are evading peril and courting adventure along with Odysseus. There aren't many readers who can still read the *Odyssey* in its original language or hear its original poetry, but everyone — children and adults alike — can still revel in this journey through the years and across the seas toward a fixed goal: toward Penelope, Telemachus, Argos, and home.

The poem ends when Odysseus takes his rightful place as husband and father (and dog owner) back at home. And it's important that it ends there. Because Odysseus at rest is Odysseus no longer. But the book is immortal because, for us readers at least, Odysseus is always on the move. ●

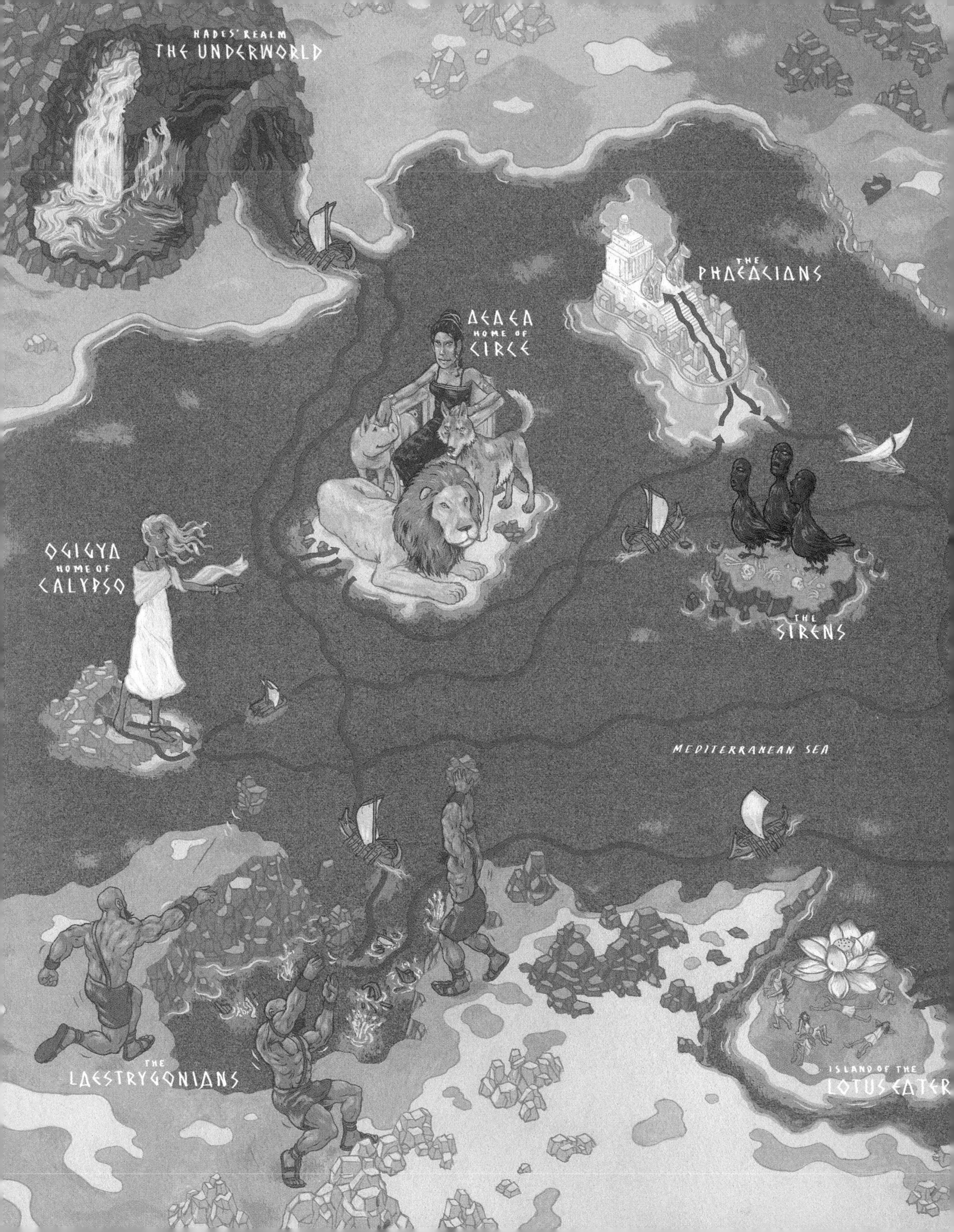

HADES' REALM
THE UNDERWORLD

THE PHAEACIANS

AEAEA
HOME OF
CIRCE

OGIGYA
HOME OF
CALYPSO

THE
SIRENS

MEDITERRANEAN SEA

THE LAESTRYGONIANS

ISLAND OF THE
LOTUS EATER

MOUNT OLYMPUS
ISMARUS
HOME OF THE
CICONES
THE TROJAN HORSE
TROY
CYLLA
AND
ARYBDIS
ITHACA
ODYSSEUS' HOME
POLYPHEMUS
THE CYCLOPS
HELIOS
AEOLUS

Elsinore

From *The Tragedy of Hamlet, Prince of Denmark*
By William Shakespeare
1603

Hamlet is one of the great masterpieces of world literature, but it is also a play that has been done to death. Even before we read it, we know its characters (Hamlet, Ophelia, The Ghost), use its words and phrases ("slings and arrows," "what dreams may come"), and recite its most famous lines ("to be or not to be," "to thine own self be true," and on and on). The degree to which the play has permeated into our culture speaks to its power, and the fact that we can still enjoy it is a testament to the play's depth — but depth and power aren't always enough to keep the play feeling fresh. It can often feel like we've seen the play a thousand times before we've seen it once.

Luckily for us, Shakespeare's play is built out of words, and these images here cannot be. We are forced to take out what is, in a way, the play's beating heart, but the result offers a fresh perspective on some things that we might normally miss — for instance, the way the play uses an increase in pace to ratchet up the drama, and its ability to light up what we might otherwise dimly imagine (a castle in sixteenth-century Denmark). It also reminds us that Shakespeare's plays are pretty simple things, really. They don't require much in the way of special effects, and with a little imagination and ingenuity all of the action can fit upon a single stage and end in around three hours. But there is no getting to the bottom of *Hamlet* because, well, there is no getting to the bottom of Hamlet. ("What a piece of work is man!")

Madness — Hamlet's madness in particular — is central to the play's deep meditation on the theme of doubt. All good plays have their share of ambiguity, but *Hamlet* is fairly unique in making that essential facet of drama the subject of the work. There is always an argument to be made for or against any given interpretation (to the point that the wisdom of the fool Polonius — "to thine own self be true," — is now printed on T-shirts and given as advice), but the two-sidedness of Hamlet is so fundamental as to be his primary characteristic. Hamlet is both deeply sane and insane, but in these maps we also get a chance to see the extent to which his madness infects the rest of the castle. He spreads like a virus, and in the end he is everywhere. (Death is everywhere as well.) His is a consuming madness.

Shakespeare's play is vivid enough on the page. These maps are an attempt to return some luster to certain aspects of the play that are hard to see from our current distance; but they can never do justice to the play's vitality, which lies entirely within its words. It's hard to believe, but there is no castle. There is no Hamlet. There is no tragedy here. It's all make-believe. But then again, Hamlet says as much himself. In a way, he restores order to the world when he commits himself to nothingness, to "the undiscovered country." And yet the irony is that through his death he achieves a real immortality. He haunts us as his father haunted him. ●

ACT I

SCENE FOUR

SCENE ONE

SCENE TWO

TO FRANCE

TO NORWAY

SCENE THREE
POLONIUS' HOUSE

ACT II

- HAMLET
- CLAUDIUS
- GERTRUDE
- OPHELIA
- POLONIUS
- REYNALDO
- ROSENCRANTZ
- GUILDENSTERN
- VOLTIMAND
- CORNELIUS
- ACTING TROUPE

SCENE TWO

FROM NORWAY

TO FRANCE

SCENE ONE
POLONIUS' HOUSE

ACT III

- HAMLET
- CLAUDIUS
- GERTRUDE
- OPHELIA
- POLONIUS
- ROSENCRANTZ
- GUILDENSTERN
- ACTING TROUPE
- POLONIUS' CORPSE
- KING'S GHOST

SCENE FOUR

SCENE TWO

SCENE ONE

SCENE THREE

ACT IV

- HAMLET
- CLAUDIUS
- GERTRUDE
- ROSENCRANTZ
- GUILDENSTERN
- FORTINBRAS
- FORTINBRAS' CAPTAIN
- OPHELIA
- LAERTES
- HORATIO
- SAILORS

SCENE THREE

SCENE ONE

SCENE FIVE

SCENE SEVEN

SCENE FOUR
A PLAIN IN DENMARK

TO ENGLAND

SCENE SIX

SCENE TWO

ACT V

- ■ HAMLET
- ▨ CLAUDIUS
- ▨ GERTRUDE
- HORATIO
- ▨ LAERTES
- GRAVE DIGGER 1
- GRAVE DIGGER 2
- OPHELIA'S CORPSE
- ▨ PRIEST
- OSRIC
- FORTINBRAS
- ENGLISH AMBASSADORS
- ↘ HAMLET'S CORPSE

SCENE ONE

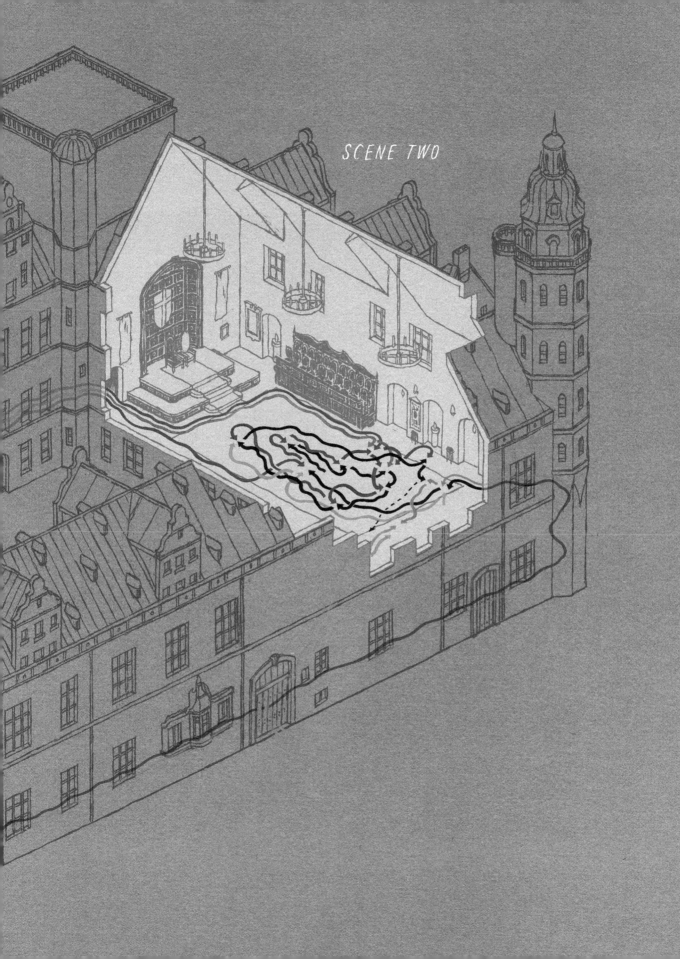

SCENE TWO

ROBINSON CRUSOE

DANIEL DEFOE

No Man Is an Island

From *Robinson Crusoe*
By Daniel Defoe
1719

Robinson Crusoe is everywhere. It's the inspiration behind space-age art films (*2001: A Space Odyssey*), young-adult dystopian hits (*Lord of the Flies*), reality TV shows (*Survivor*), radio programs ("Desert Island Discs"), primetime dramas (*Lost*), and countless other adaptations and reimaginings (*Robinson Crusoe on Mars, Cast Away, The Swiss Family Robinson*, et cetera). It's as relevant at literary symposia as it is at cocktail parties — and it offers some great tips in case you do ever find yourself stranded in nature. It's an enduring classic and an authentic, global phenomenon; and in some ways, it could hardly have come from a less likely source.

Daniel Defoe was a Puritan — and although Puritans are known for many things, thrilling entertainments are not among them. Defoe was fortunate even to be alive by the time he wrote *Robinson Crusoe*. When Defoe had turned ten years old, he'd already survived three incredible disasters: the Great Plague of London, the Great Fire of London, and the Dutch raid on the Medway. (He also spent time in the notorious Newgate Prison as an adult.) But survive he did, and before long he was thriving as an author of essays, poems, political tracts, religious pamphlets, reportage, satires, conduct manuals, and, of course, novels.

Robinson Crusoe is often cited as the first English novel, and it remains remarkable for its realism; yet despite that, *Crusoe* is rooted in an enduring fantasy. Desert islands are the stuff of childhood dreams, and seen vaguely from a great distance, it's easy to understand the enduring appeal of this vision: a pacific, pristine environment where one can tend to one's garden and proceed by one's own lights. But when that dream becomes a reality and self-reliance becomes a necessity for survival (Crusoe eventually becomes his own accountant, his own doctor, his own priest), the dream loses much of its luster. The island that Crusoe actually finds himself on is an island filled with fears and wild imaginings: beasts, cannibals, darkness, loneliness, and death. It truly is the Island of Despair.

This despair is only vanquished through Crusoe's improved knowledge — knowledge of the island, of the tactics of survival, and of himself. These maps reflect the manner in which the landscape changes according to Crusoe's own works and words (the power to name things is a real power, after all). As a result, they wind up revealing how similar the paradise that Crusoe creates is to the biblical paradise of Eden, how it even also resembles, in broad outlines, the political structures of Defoe's time (with Crusoe aspiring to the status "king"). But this is a story that is much more concerned with questions of how than it is with questions of why, and it will always be able to wriggle out of firm interpretations. It is a book that could hardly be more limited in scope (one man, one island, and one problem at a time), but it is endlessly revealing. No man is an island, but on his little island, Robinson Crusoe managed to recreate his world. •

ISLAND OF DESPAIR ————————>

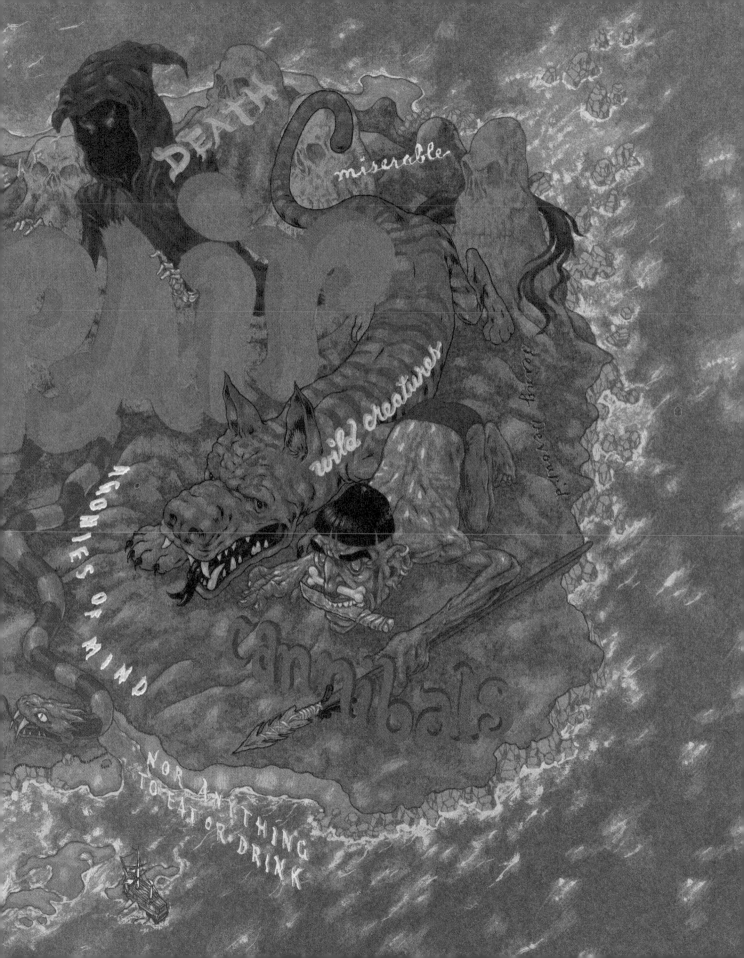

The Course of True Love

From *Pride and Prejudice*
By Jane Austen
1813

All of the books and stories included in this collection have a share of timelessness. But situated here between *Robinson Crusoe* (1719) and *A Christmas Carol* (1843), *Pride and Prejudice* (1813) seems almost shockingly contemporary. This is partly owing to the fact that so many films still take place in Victorian and Regency-era England (so we're used to living in this world, abiding by these customs, speaking in these tones); but it's the book's architecture — its form as a suspenseful love story — that makes it so eternally young. This is a story that always holds us in suspense, long after we know how it is going to end.

But the suspense of Austen's book is twofold. We care about what happens to Elizabeth not just because we care about Elizabeth, but also because we care about the entire Bennet family — and theirs is a house that does not stand upon a very firm foundation. We know about their imperiled estate almost as soon as we meet them. Wealth is status and status is integral to romance, as the book's famous opening line makes clear. And this is not just metaphor. For so long as they are romantically engaged, the characters within the novel are always navigating status as they pursue their romantic inclinations. As a result, the various families and estates are connected in deep and thoroughgoing ways, even those that might like to think of themselves as independent and above the fray. If you reside in the community, then you are a part of the community. You can escape it to the same extent that you can escape money in the modern world: That is to say, you can't.

Elizabeth Bennet's mother, Mrs. Bennet, is portrayed as something of a fool; but she is very wise in perceiving that, despite this community's apparent solidity, there is still some room for mobility, and that the way up is, almost exclusively, through family connections. The goal of the game is marriage, but the rules of the game are the rules of social etiquette. One cannot make mistakes; one cannot marry poorly.

This map shows Mrs. Bennet's world — which is also, of course, Elizabeth's. She might draw it differently if given the chance, but the connections and the ruptures, the chasms and the cracks, are never a subject of much dispute. Most people here know where (and how) they stand. Elizabeth winds up with both a good marriage *and* a good husband — something that is by no means guaranteed — but the last line of the book is dedicated not to their love for one another, but rather to their mutual love for the Gardiners, the people who "had been the means of uniting them." Marriage may seem to be the be-all and end-all, but good luck plotting a marriage alone. No, it takes a village. •

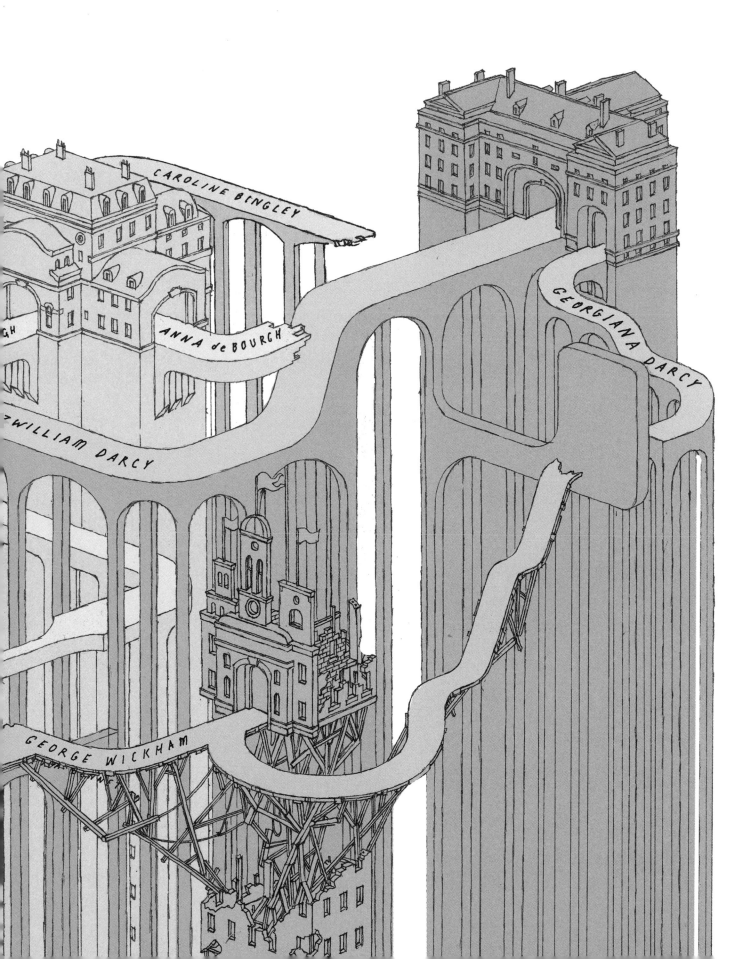

Ebenezer Scrooge: Time Traveler

From *A Christmas Carol*
By Charles Dickens
1843

A Christmas Carol is so essential to our modern idea of Christmas that it's now often hard to spot. But wherever you look, there it is. If you've ever cried during a Christmas movie (or Christmas special, or stop-motion animation, or advertisement), then you've been moved by Ebenezer Scrooge. *It's a Wonderful Life*, for instance, chose to split the character of Scrooge up into a hero (George Bailey) and a villain (Mr. Potter), but also managed to incorporate the original story's parallel universe idea. *Bad Santa*, *Elf*, and *Scrooged*, for their part, simply transformed the Scrooge character into different forms (a thief, a workaholic, and Bill Murray, respectively). Even *Die Hard* is, at its core, a redemption story, with Bruce Willis in the role of the jaded, single-minded anti-hero. And *Love Actually* can't resist the impulse to bring all of its characters back into line with their better selves by the end.

The impact and influence of *A Christmas Carol* isn't just due to the fact that it has such an archetypal redemption story; it's also owing to the fact that Dickens — no stranger to tomes — managed to pack so much into such a small space. The first edition of the book was only seventy-eight pages long, but Dickens was somehow able to include a ghost story, time travel, comedic scenes, a romance, a party, a roast goose, and, of course (the Dickens staple), a sickly, suffering child.

Like traditional Christmas carols, the book is broken up into five separate staves, showing Scrooge's progress from his meeting with Marley to Christmases past, present, future, and present again. That's a lot to cover, and yet nothing feels rushed. If anything, it feels like Scrooge's redemption comes just in time. ●

CHÁPTER ONE

■ Ebenezer Scrooge

■ The Ghost of Christmas Past

■ Fan

■ Fezziwig

■ Belle

CHAPTER TWO

Ebenezer Scrooge
The Ghost of Christmas Present
Cousin Fred
Bob Cratchit
Tiny Tim

CHAPTER THREE

■ Ebenezer Scrooge
■ The Ghost of Christmas Future
■ Bob Cratchit

CHAPTER FOUR

CHAPTER FIVE

NARRATIVE

OF THE LIFE

OF

FREDERICK
DOUGLASS

WRITTEN BY HIMSELF

Up from Slavery

From *Narrative of the Life of
Frederick Douglass, an American Slave*
By Frederick Douglass
1845

Growing up, Frederick Douglass was profoundly unfortunate in almost every respect — shipped from place to place like cargo (the dates included here show just how brutal and dehumanizing this must have been for anyone, let alone a child), and deprived of not just freedom but also of knowledge: knowledge of his father, of the date of his birth, and of the next household he was being sent to. But Douglass *was* fortunate enough to learn how to read and write. And over time, he managed to leverage that knowledge into freedom, respect, and eventually a form of real political power.

Douglass managed to find a way out and up (very quickly, too; he wrote his *Narrative* at the age of just twenty-seven), but he reminds us not to indulge too much in rejoicing over this fact. Millions of slaves never escaped, never gained such authority, and remain but poorly remembered. Douglass's book is miraculous (and wise, and sad) for all of these reasons, but it's also more than just a book. It was intended as a piece of political testimony as well as a life story. This larger purpose is evident throughout, but especially at the moment when Mr. Auld reprimanded his wife for teaching Douglass to read on the grounds that literacy would "forever unfit him to be a slave. He would at once become unmanageable, and of no value to his master."

With these words, Auld expressed a challenge to Frederick Douglass, and in his *Narrative*

Douglass takes him up on that challenge. He aims to induce empathy in people who seem to have steeled themselves against that instinct and to prove what is to them unproveable: that human beings ought not to be bought and sold. It sounds like a modest ambition. But upon publication, in resistance to that implication, people immediately doubted that Douglass had written his autobiography. They felt that a black man was unsuited for such a feat (as Auld's own words suggested they might). This doubt, this central denigration, is still cause for concern today.

Douglass heard a similar challenge to Auld's when he learned the word "abolition." He worked to make that word a reality, and his book remains a working text in confronting social injustice and the mechanisms of oppression. And thus the book extends beyond itself into Douglass's life and influence. These two maps plot the journey contained in Douglass's *Narrative*, and then show the progress of his life more broadly. They show a life lived in almost perpetual exile (a sort of diaspora of freed African Americans) and in support of a profoundly just cause. They also contain a geography that is in many ways quite familiar. The rural, agricultural look of the Eastern Seaboard of the 1830s does not blind us to the familiar American landscape. This really happened here — that point is worth remembering. ●

APE TO NEW YORK

Mason-Dixon Line

RENAMING HIMSELF, FREDERICK DOUGLASS BEGINS HIS CAREER AS AN ORATOR AND ABOLISHIONIST IN NEW BEDFORD, MA.

BAY

MARYLAND'S Eastern Shore

COLONEL LLOYD'S GREAT HOUSE FARM WYE, MD

1822

N.J.

DELAWARE a slave state

BORN 1817 OR 1818 TALBOT COUNTY AND GIVEN THE NAME "FREDERICK AUGUSTUS WASHINGTON BAILEY"

N
W   E
S

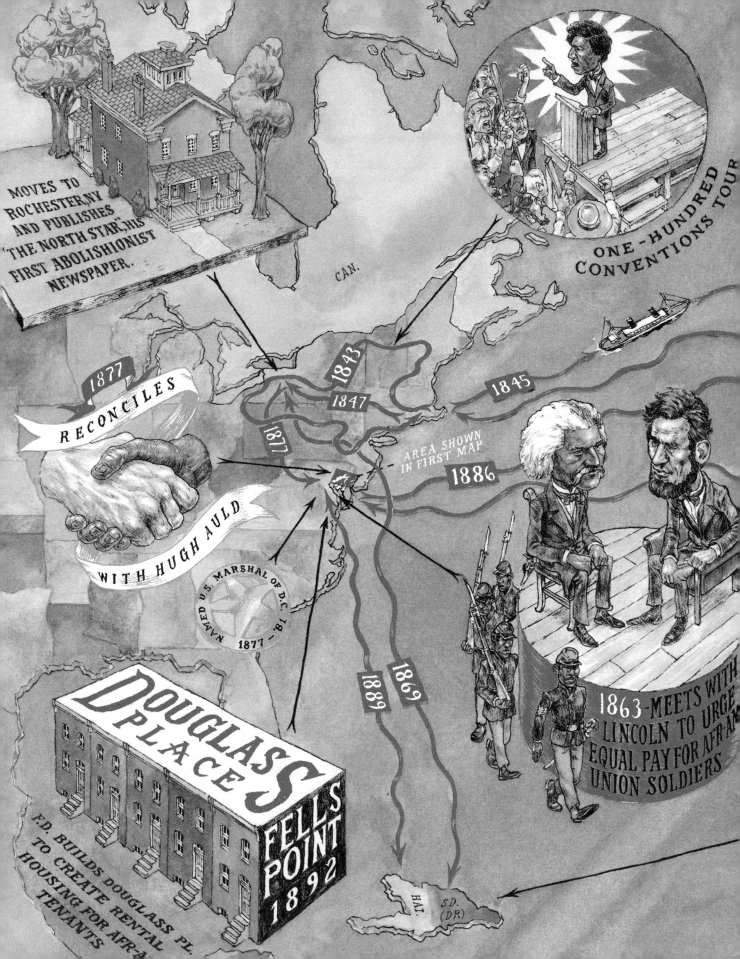

MOVES TO ROCHESTER, NY AND PUBLISHES "THE NORTH STAR," HIS FIRST ABOLISHIONIST NEWSPAPER.

ONE-HUNDRED CONVENTIONS TOUR

CAN.

1843

1847

1845

1877

RECONCILES

1877

WITH HUGH AULD

NAMED U.S. MARSHAL OF D.C. 1877

AREA SHOWN IN FIRST MAP

1886

1863 - MEETS WITH LINCOLN TO URGE EQUAL PAY FOR AFR-AM UNION SOLDIERS

1889 1869

DOUGLASS PLACE

FELLS POINT 1892

F.D. BUILDS DOUGLASS PL. TO CREATE RENTAL HOUSING FOR AFR-AM TENANTS

HAI. S.D. (DR)

SCO.

IRE.

ENG.

1846

FRA.

1887

ATLANTIC OCEAN

ITA.

GR.

EGY.

DOUGLASS SPENDS HIS FINAL YEARS AT HIS "CEDAR HILL" HOME IN D.C. HE CONTINUED HIS FIGHT FOR EQUAL RIGHTS FOR AFRICAN-AMERICANS AND WOMEN. HE IS BURIED IN ROCHESTER, N.Y.

1818 - 1895

1869 COMMITTEE TO ANNEX SANTO DOMINGO

U.S. MINISTER TO HAITI 1889

N
W   E
S

The Pequod and Its Quarry

From *Moby Dick; or, The Whale*
By Herman Melville
1851

Moby Dick is almost beyond interpretation at this point. The work itself is oceanic, comically large in scope and ambition; and although it has been rendered into poetry, film, music, visual art, and more, none of these adaptations have come close to settling the question of the book's ultimate meaning (which, in this way, can be seen as the reading public's own white whale). And as a result, in trying to map this great work, we've set aside Nantucket and the sprawling seas and focused instead on the two main combatants: the whaling ship and the whale. This takes us out of space and time and places us instead inside the *things* of the novel. Because metaphor is everywhere in *Moby Dick*, but metaphor is contained within the stuff that surrounds us (or did, in mid-nineteenth century America): in boats, the sea, industry, and oil.

People tend to talk about animate and inanimate things as though the dividing line between them is quite clear, but in Melville's universe "being" is a porous state. The Pequod may lack a heart, but it comes alive at sea. It also quickly reveals itself to be at odds with the sea over which it travels. After all, the ship is a place where the sea's most inscrutable and glorious creatures — its whales — are denatured and transformed into oil.

The Pequod, in fact, is most alive when it is most dominant over the environment that surrounds it. After a whale has been taken, every man aboard finds his role. The ship rests confidently upon the waves, and the whale is hoisted up, butchered, harvested, and discarded. It takes some time for the whale's blubber to be converted into valuable oil, but from the moment that the whale is brought on board the ship, it has ceased to be a whale and become instead a commodity. The living ship thus extracts the life from the living seas. It seems fair to say that one of the many concerns of *Moby Dick* is the question of being, of soul, of spirit. Over the years, throughout its many hunts and harvests, the Pequod has become less and less ship and more and more whale. It is composed of whalebone and ivory as well as wood. And it tends, inevitably (and increasingly, as the novel progresses), back toward the sea. The ship *is* the world (as a seaman seems to imply in the chapter "The Ship"), but of course, the ship is also, at times, no more than a speck on the horizon, a vanishing thing. It is all a matter of perspective. And sometimes a ship is just a ship. But when a ship has the power to turn the Leviathan into the stuff that lights our lamps (or did), then it's hard not to see something miraculous even in its smallest part. As for the whale, well, it's important to see where human knowledge stops. To name is not to know. Melville may well break down the ship and the whale for our benefit, but in the end we're all confronting an implacable, immutable truth. We cannot know this whale. In this respect, the story never ends. ●

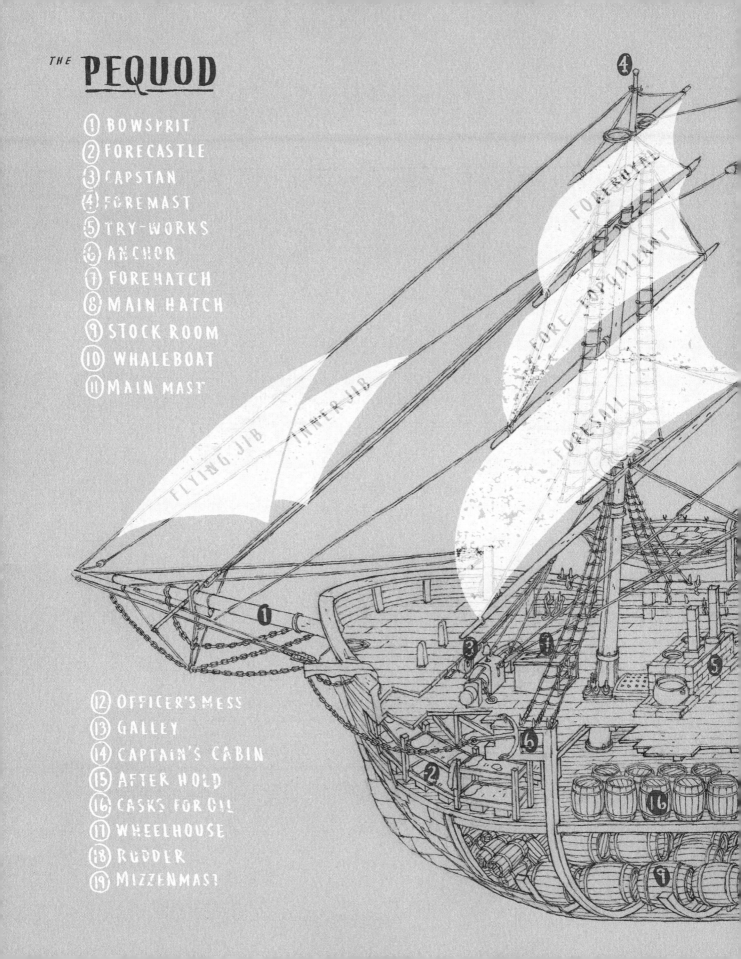

THE PEQUOD

LARGEST RECORDED SPERM WHALES: 65'–70'

① FLUKE
② FLENSING SPIRAL
③ BLUBBER (TRYED FOR OIL)
④ MUSCLE OR MEAT (DISCARDED)
⑤ LUNGS
⑥ DIGESTIVE TRACT
⑦ AMBERGRIS (USED IN PERFUME)

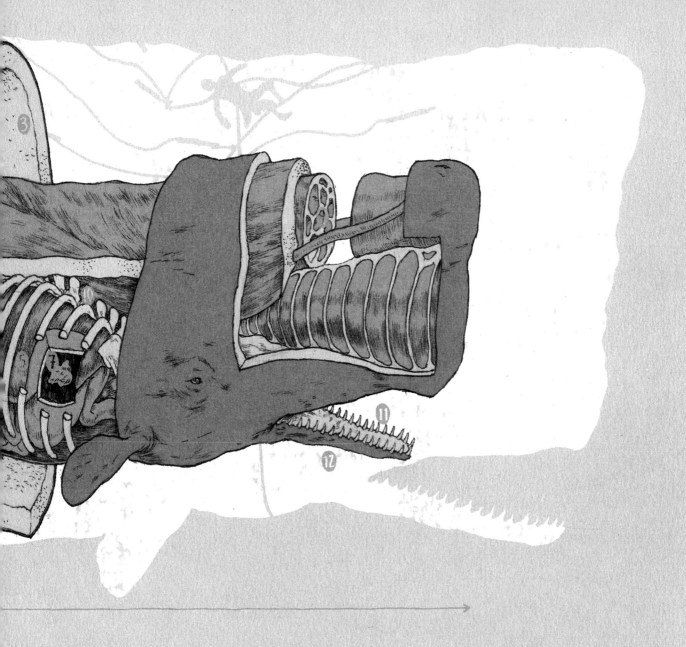

MELVILLE'S MOBY DICK: 90'+

⑧ JUNK (OR MELON)
⑨ TUN OR SPERMACETI ORGAN (USED FOR OIL)
⑩ WHALEBONE
⑪ IVORY TEETH
⑫ JAW (USED FOR CARVING)
⑬ THE CASE

A Narrow Fellow in the Grass

EMILY DICKINSON

Route Zero

From "A Narrow Fellow in the Grass"
By Emily Dickinson
ca. 1865

When Emily Dickinson's poem was first published in 1865, it was on account of her sister-in-law. Dickinson did not seek publication herself (or provide a title for the work, which was then called "The Snake"), but that's not to say she didn't appreciate the ostensible favor. Dickinson was, however, displeased at the edits that were made to her already finished product. The removal of a question mark (after the question, "did you not?") might not rattle the average Joe, but for Dickinson, every word and every punctuation mark was vital and considered.

"A Narrow Fellow in the Grass" is as vivid and sensual a poem as you are ever likely to find, but its central topic — the snake itself — is unstated and only ever uncertainly seen. And yet, there it is: always mobile, always shifting, but always there. To follow it is to follow evidence, not proof. And as a result of this ambiguity, our senses remain heightened and our minds alert. The poem calls to mind the snake (the metaphor as well as the animal) in all its aspects because it does not insist on any single aspect in particular. The question mark remains.

When we take a photograph, we often describe the act as "capturing a moment," but that phrase fails to express the fact that our "moments" in the present extend back into the past as well — sometimes even taking us beyond our human existence to the realm of instinct, to a knowledge that is shared and unshakeable. This poem captures its own moment in a much more inclusive and comprehensive fashion. It is a moment that is unified neither in space nor in time; but its message is coherent, and its insight is acute. We hear the rumor of danger, feel the rustle of the grass, plunge instinctively into our shared, secret knowledge, and then are left trembling. In an instant we move from a jangle of sensory input to "zero at the bone." We never travel anywhere; we remain where we are. We are rooted to our knowledge, which is as instantaneous as it is deep.

Emily Dickinson has a reputation as a morbid, isolated poet. But her words bring us to life with the force of an electric shock, and the result plunges us into bright colors and deep feeling. But there is also darkness here. The thing that we seek, the mystery of the poem, the unnamed subject itself, is important to remember. It is like a midnight knock at the door. It comes from silence, ends in silence, and rips us from our slumber. We are awake now, even if we can't quite grasp what it was that woke us.

(Also, for fans of *The Mighty Boosh*, it's hard not to wonder what Emily Dickinson might have done with the character of Bob Fossil, the zookeeper who calls the zoo's snake "the windy man," or, alternatively, "the long mover." But that's a question for another day.) ●

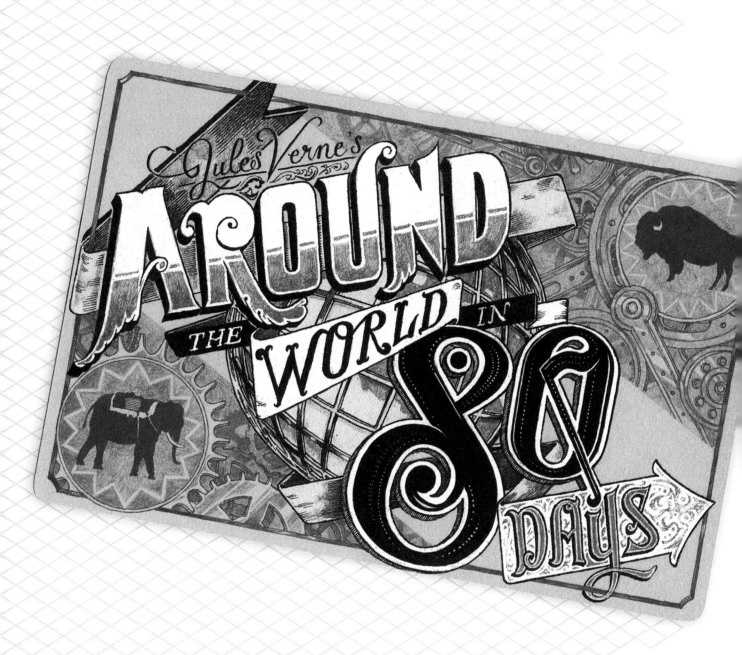

Phileas Fogg's Incredibly Credible Circumnavigation

From *Around the World in Eighty Days*
By Jules Verne
1873

Few works of fiction are as geographically oriented as *Around the World in Eighty Days*. What's interesting about the book, however, isn't the actual geography involved — indeed, the cities and countries involved in Phileas Fogg's travels are still quite recognizable to us now, almost 150 years later — but rather the way that Verne forced Victorian readers to reimagine what this geography meant. He took a world that still seemed enormous — with plains that stretched for days and seas that took months to cross — and made a convincing case that humans already had the technology to make the world a much smaller place.

Jules Verne was initially inspired by a newspaper article (or so the story goes) about traveling around the globe. Clearly, he grasped the right idea at the right time. Someone *could* do it in such a short amount of time, especially with railroads recently built across America and India; but up to that point, no one had. It was a time when the optimism of the burgeoning technological age seemed almost to be running behind the technology. It was a world where telegraph lines and steamboats were fueling the British Empire 2.0, and it would eventually pave the way for the global society we live in today. What the time period lacked was an evangelist for this brave new world. And by stacking his work of science fiction with scientific facts, Verne managed both to thrill and to persuade in equal measure.

Readers of the serialized novel took Verne's words so seriously that bets were even placed on the question (which seemed real enough) of whether the fictional Fogg would actually arrive in time. Before the century was out, daredevil journalist Nellie Bly took up Fogg's challenge and managed to finish the trip with two days to spare. It was official: the future had arrived.

Just as Verne took care to deal with the reality of transportation technology at the time of writing, we too have taken care to represent the vehicles as they really were (at least as far as we were able). But the primary thrill of this book lies not in verisimilitude but rather in Phileas Fogg's passionate chase of a technocratic dream. His days are numbered here as he spans continents and overcomes an almost endless series of obstacles (not to say treacheries). As in so many other travel stories, the journey ends at the same place where the journey began; but as with so many other travel stories, everything has changed in the meantime. The London where Fogg completes his circumnavigation is part of a different world entirely. ●

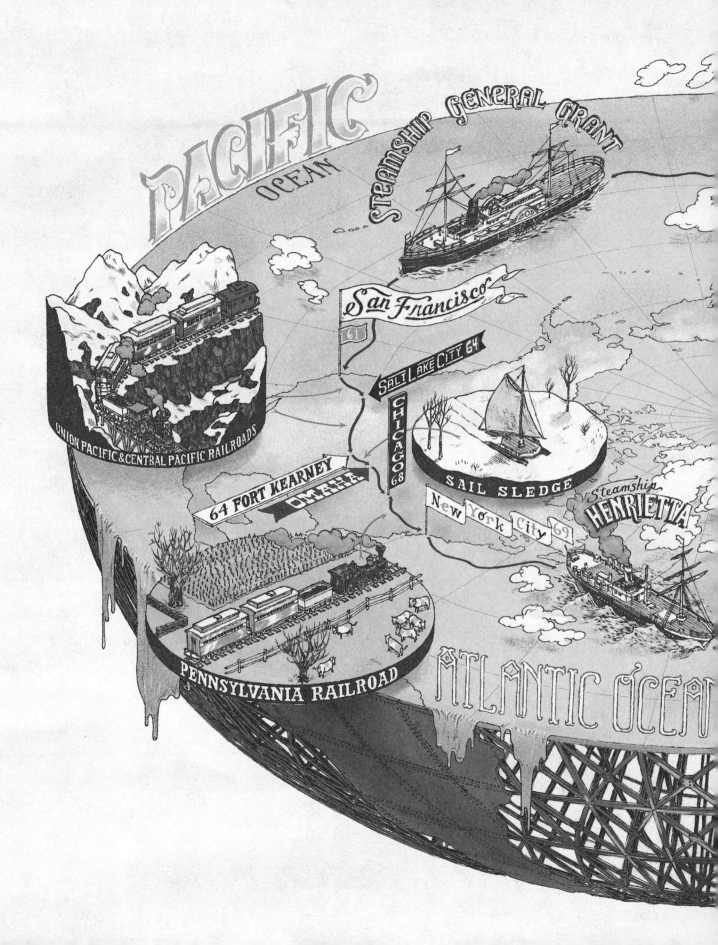

Huckleberry Finn's Mississippi River Journey

From *Adventures of Huckleberry Finn*
By Mark Twain
1884

America may be the *land* of the free, but the two leading contenders for the title of "great American novel" actually take place on the water. For Melville, the ocean contained all of humanity's great secrets (and metaphors); but for Twain, it was the water itself that was the key. In *Adventures of Huckleberry Finn*, the river is both the setting of the novel and its central theme. And the fact that it also paved the way (so to speak) for the American road movie is just an added bonus.

Although Huck Finn was born in a children's book (namely, *The Adventures of Tom Sawyer*), his own story is not for kids. But like so many children's books, *Adventures of Huckleberry Finn* is deeply concerned with morality. Its metaphors and characters interact so organically that it's often easy to forget that the river really exists. It is always changing yet always right there, and always in tension with itself. But Twain's river (and, because he was a former riverboat pilot, it really was his river) is something more American than this enduring ancient symbol.

The Mississippi is a river that literally divides our nation. It's a river that, for Jim, is the only road to freedom, and it only runs one way: toward the slave-holding states. And with every mile that Huck and Jim travel south, the more perilous their journey becomes. But this is a comedy as well as a tragedy (with the tragedy mostly taking place off-stage), and as a result,

the more danger they encounter, the more outlandish the scenarios become.

As with so many great stories, danger lurks around every bend, but it is people who are the trouble, and most of the people are on land. Life on the river is thus "free and easy and comfortable." It's an oasis in every way. Once the pair passes Cairo, however, it's hard not to view the antebellum South as some sort of asylum for the ignorant and insane. On all sides, the two are surrounded by hucksters, racists, zealots, bloody-minded aristocrats, and simple-minded fools. Early on, Tom Sawyer accuses Huck of having no imagination, but it is Huck's role as skeptic and arbitrator that illuminates the book and the people around him. Always being grappled with by people on both sides, he stays in the middle. He defines his own morality, makes his own course, and continues on.

This map attempts to borrow Huck's wisdom and follows the river just as Twain presents it: as a simple trail of water, heading in a single direction, which nevertheless is full of endless complexity and confusion. Sometimes a river is just a river; but at other times, it's certainly not. After all, if you've gotten to the bottom of the Mississippi River, then you're probably dead; and if you think you've heard the last word on Huckleberry Finn, then you've probably stopped listening. Rivers aren't rivers when they stop moving. ●

An Education

From "A Report to an Academy"
By Franz Kafka
1917

No one would call Franz Kafka a kid-friendly writer exactly, but his works have a lot in common with children's books. Like them, Kafka's works possess a profound simplicity of vision and rely in large part on humor for their emotional impact. But there are also times when Kafka's stories and novels engage with the central, and essentially childish, question of who we are, what our nature truly is. And this question is as proper to humans as it is to Babe the sheep-pig.

Red Peter begins his "report" by declaring that "it is now nearly five years since I was an ape," but insisting that his distance from that state is identical with that of the humans in attendance. He cannot become an ape again any more than they can. We are eerily proximate to our prehistory here, but with the blunt tool of language we cannot quite grasp it. We can, however, begin to draw a line ("the line an erstwhile ape has had to follow in entering and establishing himself in the world of men"). Or, at least, Red Peter can. He has traveled that line. It is a journey from unconsciousness to consciousness, from pre-language to language, and it offers us everything while telling us nothing about what we want to know.

This is a survival tale stripped down to its barest details. When Peter, injured and insulted, is imprisoned in his cage, he knows only one thing: "no way out." No physical way out, anyway (Red Peter pointedly refuses to use the word "freedom"), but the will to live drives him to seek "any" way as opposed to none. And here is where the continuous line that he draws splits dramatically apart. Red Peter is forced to live, "Yet as far as Hagenbeck was concerned, the place for apes was in front of a locker — well then, I had to stop being an ape."

Red Peter does not say that he achieved this change in an instant, but there is no way to account for the birth of consciousness. He points to the discrete moments — the sense of imprisonment, the desire to get out, the pipe, the bottle, and the word ("Hallo!") — but he cannot take us with him on his journey. It is past and gone forever. He can, however, reflect on what it is that he has achieved from a new and unique perspective. And as it was for Adam and Eve, so it is for Peter: There is a price to pay. As he puts it, "One learns when one needs a way out; one learns at all costs."

The best way out is any way out, and the only way out is humanity's, so Peter takes what is available to him. But his unspoken past remains — in his mind, as in his mate ("a half-trained little chimpanzee and I take comfort from her as apes do") — and this unspeakable yet deeply felt knowledge reminds us that consciousness itself is not an answer. In fact, it might be better to say that consciousness is the entryway into the trial that is our lives. And as Peter suggests through his willingness to take his trousers down to show "the plain truth," his effort, like ours, remains fundamentally absurd. (This is, in the end, the story of a talking ape after all.) ●

Fig. 1

Fig. 2

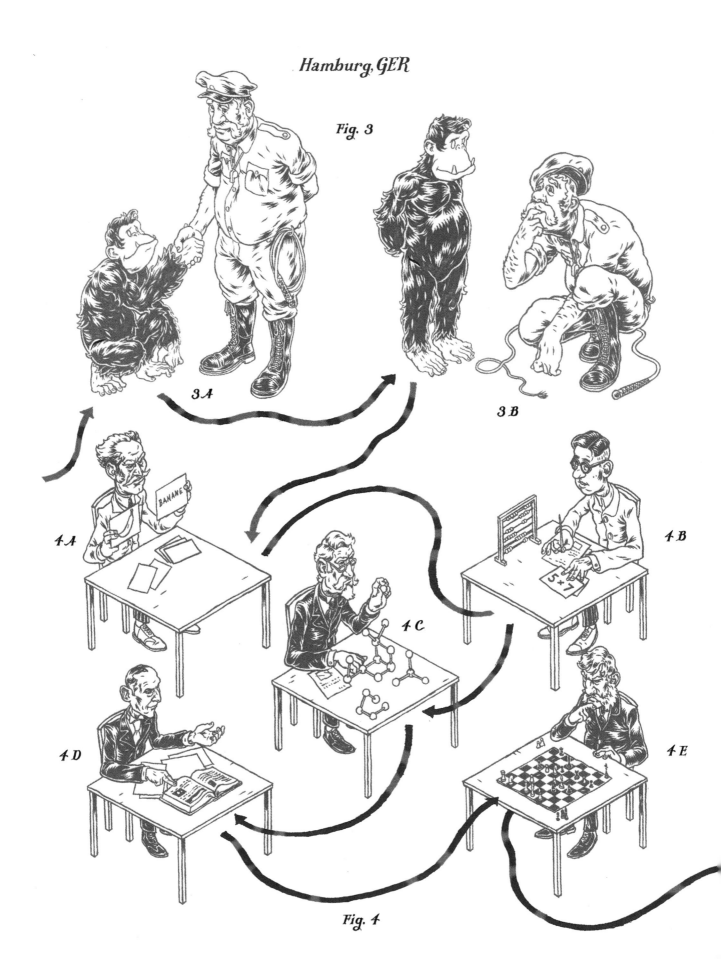

Hamburg, GER

Fig. 3

3 A

3 B

4 A

4 B

4 C

4 D

4 E

Fig. 4

Fig. 5

Infinite Intelligence

From "The Library of Babel"
By Jorge Luis Borges
1941

Hell has been imagined in a nearly infinite number of ways, but in all of these endless variations — from *The Epic of Gilgamesh* to *The Inferno* to *Bill and Ted's Bogus Journey* — hell is always (and forever) a landscape, an environment, a place. Or, as Borges puts it: "The Universe (which others call the Library) is composed of an indefinite number of hexagonal galleries... one after another, endlessly." It is this sense of geographic burden, the idea of always being *here*, that allows "The Library of Babel" to function as both a philosophical essay and an existential horror story.

Although the story is delivered in the style of an instruction manual (one that is surprisingly hard to follow, it should be said), there is also a thrilling pace to it, as the true nature of this world is revealed in layers. First we encounter the individual cell ("hexagonal galleries, with vast air shafts between, surrounded by very low railings"); then the knowable world for a typical librarian ("I am preparing to die just a few leagues from the hexagon in which I was born"); and only then do we get the God's eye view of this entire universe ("The Library is total... its shelves register all possible combinations"). It all sounds so straightforward, but complexity and paradox are infused throughout. The original, simple-sounding cell is actually quite difficult to imagine (or recreate, in this case). And despite the incredible size of this universe, it is, on a human scale, cramped and claustrophobic ("there are two very small closets. In the first, one may

sleep standing up"). But these details do not get us any closer to comprehension. Infinity itself is full of paradoxes. And Borges, in these few pages, is constantly shifting our perspective, taking us to the brink of things and throwing us off. Like the librarians of his story, the human mind forever teeters on the brink when it comes to questions of the infinite.

As Borges teases out the implications of his library, Borges's skills as a philosopher are immediately evident; but he was also a writer, and as the story closes, the focus shifts again, as the nightmarish depths of this world expand to take on the emotional fears of the author as well. After all, this is a world that contains *all* books, and as a result, any one book that an author may write is of vanishing importance. The clearest, loveliest, wisest volume takes its place among the shelves, as does the volume containing a repeating series of M's, C's, and V's. Our narrator holds out hope that order, at least, is present here. But as with all things at the Library, that dream is double-edged, as it is that same order that will allow his body to fall, unobstructed, to his grave in "the fathomless air." These maps, in some ways, require little imagination. Borges's words have already created this world, but even when confined on four sides it remains perilously easy to go plunging into the abysses it implies. Man, the imperfect librarian, can never rest easily here.

There are no arrows on this map because, as readers, we are everywhere and nowhere.●

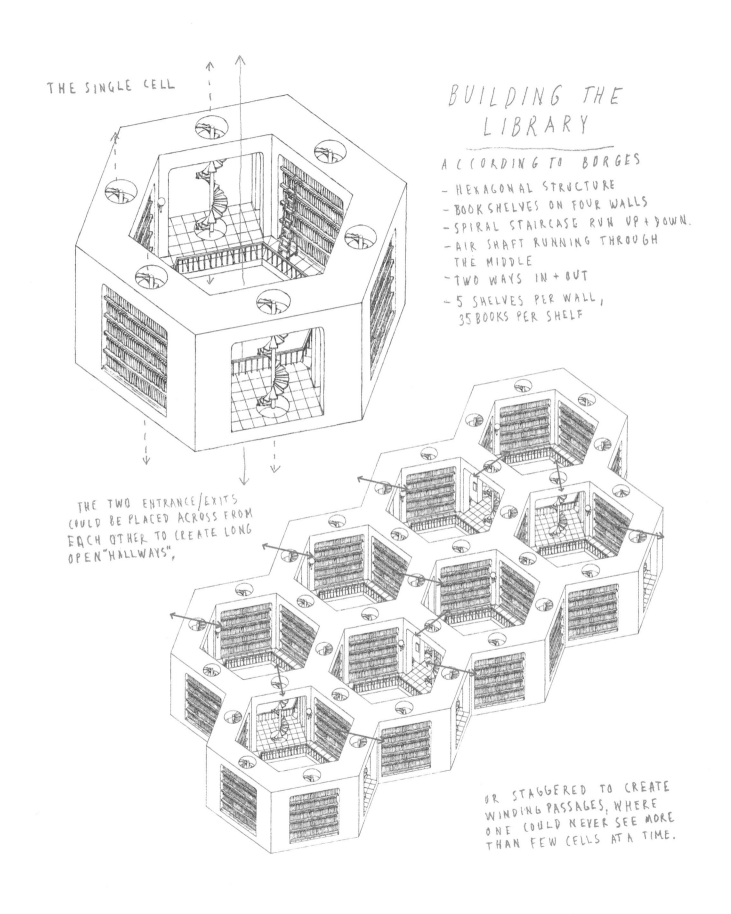

THE SINGLE CELL

BUILDING THE LIBRARY

ACCORDING TO BORGES
- HEXAGONAL STRUCTURE
- BOOK SHELVES ON FOUR WALLS
- SPIRAL STAIRCASE RUN UP + DOWN.
- AIR SHAFT RUNNING THROUGH THE MIDDLE
- TWO WAYS IN + OUT
- 5 SHELVES PER WALL, 35 BOOKS PER SHELF

THE TWO ENTRANCE/EXITS COULD BE PLACED ACROSS FROM EACH OTHER TO CREATE LONG OPEN "HALLWAYS".

OR STAGGERED TO CREATE WINDING PASSAGES, WHERE ONE COULD NEVER SEE MORE THAN FEW CELLS AT A TIME.

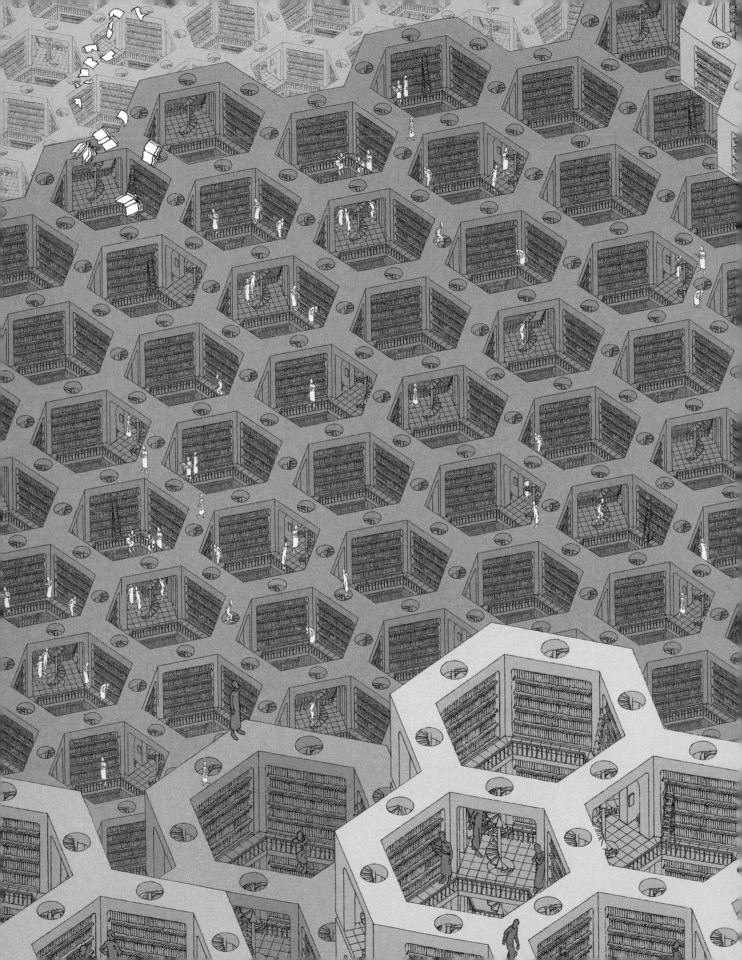

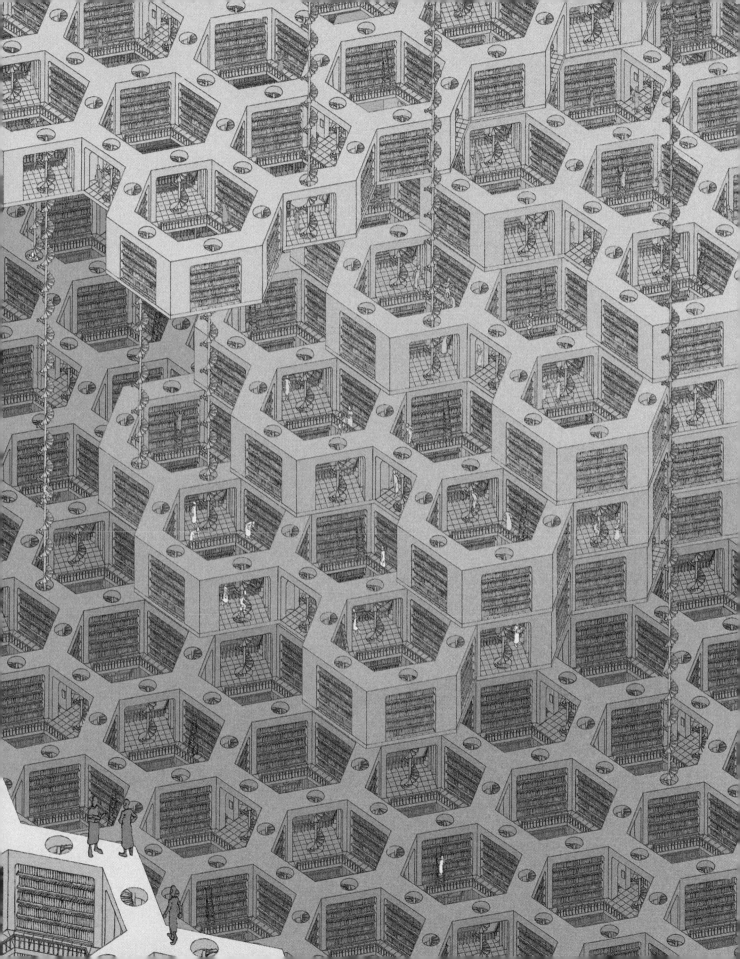

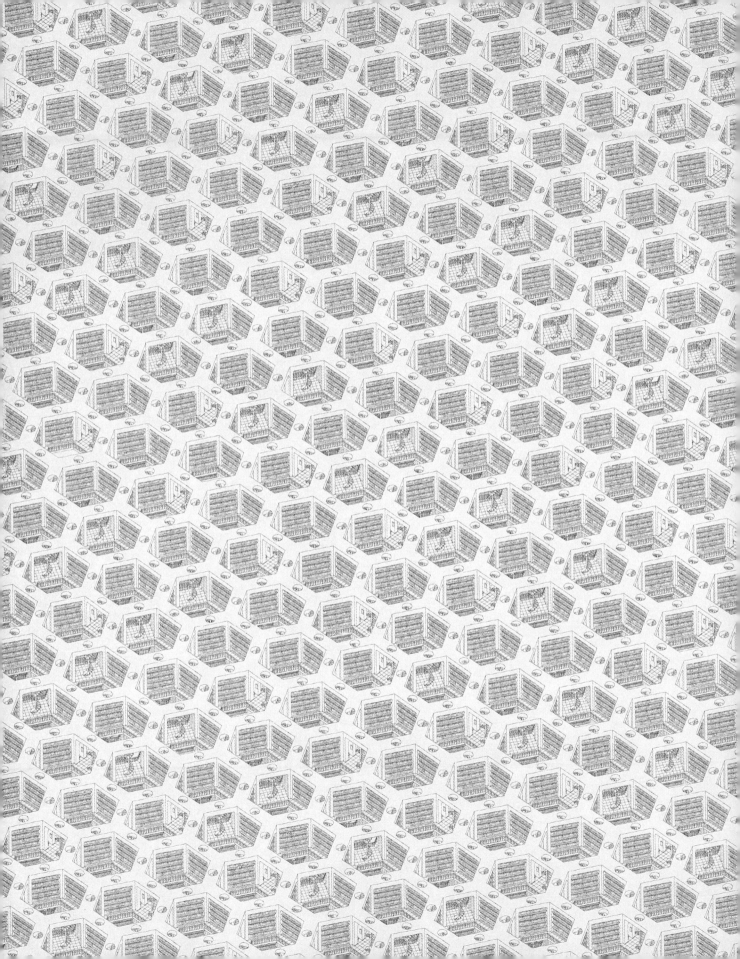

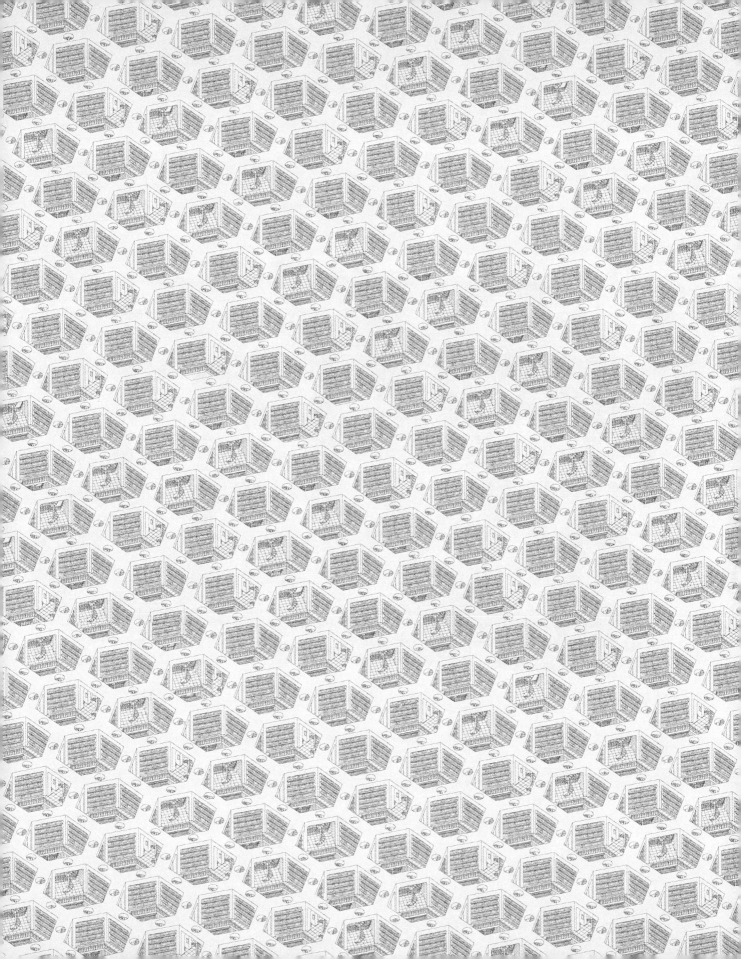

Converging Paths

From "The Lottery"
By Shirley Jackson
1948

"The Lottery" is almost as famous for its reception as it is for its contents. After it was published in *The New Yorker* in 1948, the magazine received a barrage of letters and calls. People were furious with Jackson for bringing such darkness into their lives. But many stories are dark. (H.P. Lovecraft had only died ten years before, after all.) Something else was happening here. Something that perhaps could best be described as "uncanny."

We recognize the town in "The Lottery" and accept it without hesitation. It is a typical, familiar place, filled with typical, familiar names: Adams, Allen, Bentham, Clark, Dunbar, Graves, Hutchinson. And although we sense that something here is rotten, the manner in which we as readers tend to discover this story — in a prestigious weekly magazine, in a library, or in a freshman English class — makes the reveal just that much more shocking. And no matter how many times we read it, the shock always comes. This crime should not be happening. Not here. And yet we also know that it couldn't happen any other way.

A black spot indicates the sacrificial victim. But that black spot infects and implicates everyone in this unnamed town, killers and killed alike. And it implicates us as well. In the same way that a certain level of abstraction allows us to project ourselves into characters and concepts (like Mickey Mouse, love, clouds, et cetera), this town's blank demeanor and nondescript patronymics force us to consider the ways in which we unintentionally (not to say unwillingly) subscribe to thousands of lesser crimes against our neighbors. The German word for uncanny is *unheimliche* — the negative expression of *heimliche*, or "homely." We are both profoundly at home here and yet profoundly not at home. And so we write our letters insisting that this is not us, this is not where we live, this is not who we are. But we tend to protest a bit too much. This book remains hugely popular in schools (when it's not banned) for exactly this reason.

But to say that "The Lottery" means such-and-such or condemns so-and-so is to miss the true source of its power. This town is not named. This place is not visible on a map. And the trajectories of the various characters can only really be understood in relation to the ultimate tragedy here. They all converge on the black spot because those are the rules and that is what these people do and that is what they have always done. This is the nature of their community, and once that black spot is eradicated the community loses its coherence and disappears. What that black spot "means" means less than the fact that it is there at all. In the meantime, we will continue to write our letters and ban our books. We are not them, we promise. ●

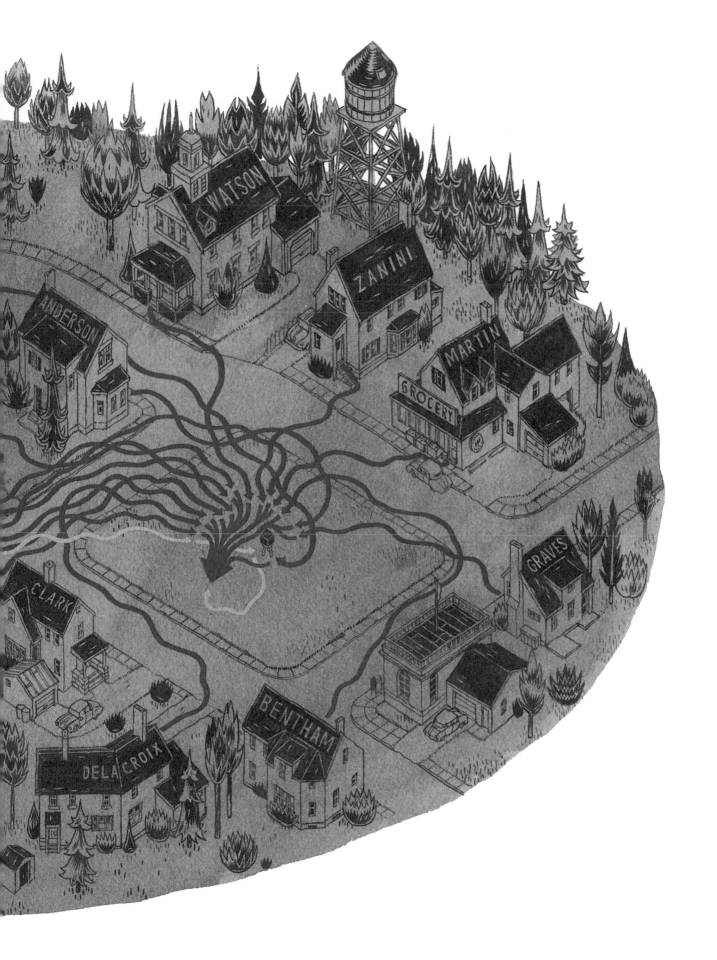

Journey to Nowhere

From *Invisible Man*
By Ralph Ellison
1952

Aside from perhaps Benjamin Franklin and Frederick Douglass, it's hard to think of an American figure who has participated more fully in American life than Ralph Ellison. Born into relative poverty in Oklahoma City in 1914, Ellison was able to attend a good school and had people around him who encouraged his interests in music, literature, and technology. (Throughout his life he remained an endlessly curious human being.) He attended the Tuskegee Institute on a music scholarship, but left the school to head to New York in 1936. Once there, he quickly became familiar with Alan Locke, Langston Hughes, and Richard Wright, and began writing and publishing book reviews at Wright's suggestion. His career had begun.

During his time in Depression-era New York, Ellison also worked with the Living Lore Unit (part of the Federal Writers Project) on gathering urban folklore, and began work on some fiction projects as well. During World War II, he worked in the kitchen of a merchant marine ship, and at war's end he began work on *Invisible Man*, which won the National Book Award for fiction the following year. He wasn't done, of course, and taught, wrote, traveled, and lectured until his death in 1994; but *Invisible Man* remains, by far, his masterpiece. Ellison has much in common with his main character, and his book draws heavily from American art and culture of the time. But the book itself weaves influence and inspiration together so adeptly that the resulting work is something entirely startling and unique. It is, without a doubt, a great American novel (and speaks to the fact that it's unreasonable ever

to talk of one such champion) — but it's also an American tragedy. Huckleberry Finn finds himself on the river by book's end; Ishmael rises again from the sea after the Pequod sinks; but our narrator here ends where he begins: invisible still, and underground.

Tragedy, then, may not be quite the word, as tragedies require a fall. Ellison's narrator does not fall so much as he abides, and his "flaw" is not his own. He is not invisible, but others make him so. In "Notes from Underground," Dostoevsky's anti-hero lives underground in an exclusively metaphorical sense. His psyche is what lies beneath (a fact in which he finds a perverse elation). Ellison's underground is literal, though it has similarly large metaphorical implications. In America, the Underground Railroad served as a route to freedom — but freedom wasn't guaranteed, and the manner of survival that it offered in the meantime was imperiled and oppressed. It was born of a lack of other opportunities. And here, in Ellison's hands, that underground has become real — and permanent.

The liberation that life underground offers to our narrator is a liberation of voice. His underground dwelling, like Dostoevsky's underground of the mind, is a place of greater truth. But the vitality of the world aboveground, a place both black and white, with heroes, villains, cowards, and a teeming mass of people and life, is something that will always draw us out. The lights burn brightly underground — all 1,369 of them — but they offer a sadly artificial flame. Like the song on the record player, they offer a lament. ●

THE SOUTH

HOME

① GRADUATION SPEECH

② BATTLE ROYAL

③ NARRATOR'S HOME

④ DREAMS GRANDFATHER'S CURSE

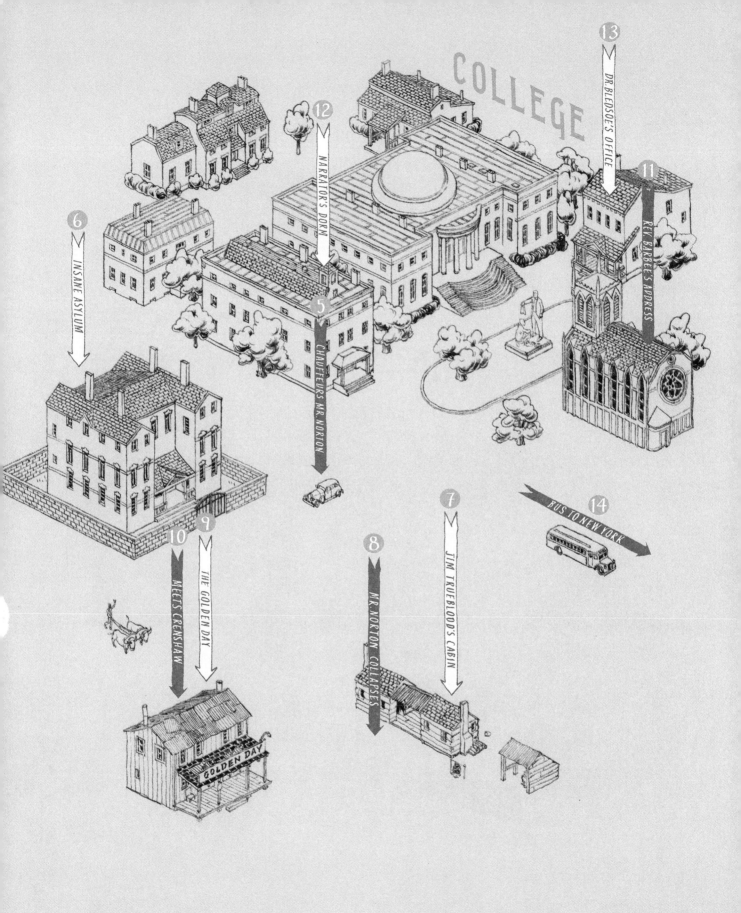

The Waiting Room

From *Waiting for Godot*
By Samuel Beckett
1953

Humans are small, but ideas are big. That is somewhat inspirational, but it's also something of a design flaw. Our minds outpace ourselves, and then, before we know it, we arrive at the universal, the all-encompassing, the absolute. Before we know it, we come face-to-face with Elohim, Allah, Buddah, Jehovah, God, and... Godot? Or do we? Historically speaking, it's hard to deny that these deities (or this deity, depending on one's outlook) appear quickly and consistently wherever humans congregate, but are these truly gods that we encounter, or are they simply concepts? This simple question (which often serves as a punchline) is central to Beckett's iconic play. But there's also much more to it than that. (Thank God.)

As the Gospel of John famously relates, "In the beginning was the Word, and the Word was with God, and the Word was God." But words (to say nothing of God — Old Testament or New) are deceitful things. They are full of connotation and promise but are also nearly impossible to capture in their entirety. Godot, for its part (or his? hers?), is a meaningless word, but as a name it is beyond poignant. We hear the echo of "I am" in the name of this figure who is destined to be forever without. His name appears as a kind of covenant. But then again, he is not here. Like all the faithful everywhere, we remain in wait.

Godot is as loud as he is distant. We are small beside the enormity of what we imagine him to be (even should he prove nonexistent). And we heed our imaginings of Godot even as reality (via time, for instance, and the changing of the seasons) imposes itself upon the stage. Pozzo leads Lucky in the beginning, and Lucky leads Pozzo at the end. The circular nature of time itself echoes the circularity (not to say solipsism) of human thought. There are some distant, cultural resonances — of the Sphynx and the ages of man, for instance — but this is also *the* play of modernism. It is bare in the extreme, and urgent.

The play is words and little else (a tree here, a bowler hat there), but it is also a living document. This is a play about the thing that we are waiting for. And it's a reminder that waiting is, in itself, an escape. Godot — like the idea of Godot, like the hint of Godot, like the shadow of Godot — remains a threat. To flee him is to live, but then the question remains: to live for what? (Good luck answering that one.) •

Flannery O'Connor's Family Vacation

From "A Good Man Is Hard to Find"
By Flannery O'Connor
1953

In cinematic terms, "A Good Man Is Hard to Find" is an ensemble piece. It has no main character to speak of, just as it has no "good man" at its core. What we get instead is a ragtag bunch of self-involved mediocrities: a grandmother who acts like a child (and who finds her equal in her grandchildren); a son, Bailey, who lacks the strength to resist either his mother or his presumed executioners; and a killer who seems to resent his past as much as he reviles the present. As far as family vacations go, this is a bad one.

"A Good Man Is Hard to Find," like "The Lottery" (see page 91), is a staple of high school English classes. This makes sense. Both of the stories are haunting, incriminating, and deeply ambiguous. But the ironic fact (given the authors' divergent religious inclinations) is that while Jackson's story seems to speak to a sort of original sin, O'Connor's fable hones in on a particularly American crime. O'Connor's story is told with a blandness that heightens the banality of its various evils. This blandness is shocking, given the story's content, but it is also apt. The family's utter lack of interest in the moral component of America's history is echoed in the amoral tone of the narration; in the way the family car glides past the Civil War monument; in the "joke" that the grandmother tells; and in the anecdotes that The Misfit relays. These characters are not interested in ethics or morals, but this remains a deeply moral tale.

The journey of "A Good Man" is a journey through the American South, and the goal is a plantation of the mind — the grandmother's mind, as it happens. Her memory, in fact, is one of the most reliable clues that this story will end badly, despite its blandness. The revelation of the memory's falsehood is provided in ominous fits in starts, but in the end we learn the truth: The plantation in question does not exist, and the resulting wrong-turn takes our less-than-beloved family into a far deeper reckoning than they ever anticipated.

The grandmother sets the stage for this final reckoning in her conversation at Red Sammy's. This is where the "good man" makes his appearance. We see remnants of this good man's faded glory in the idealization of the plantation, in the grandmother's recollections of "better times," and in the notion of "good blood." The grandmother, with her progeny behind her, refuses to believe that The Misfit, a man who looks and sounds like the kind of people she grew up with, could be a cruel sadist. As she puts it, "Why you're one of my babies!"

Although O'Connor has her finger on the pulse of the 1950s here, her story is also noteworthy for its understanding of place. After all, it isn't hard to follow this family. Their starting point is known and their destination is not far away. ("It took them twenty minutes to reach the outskirts of the city.") Then as now, Misfits abound, and good men are hard to find. ●

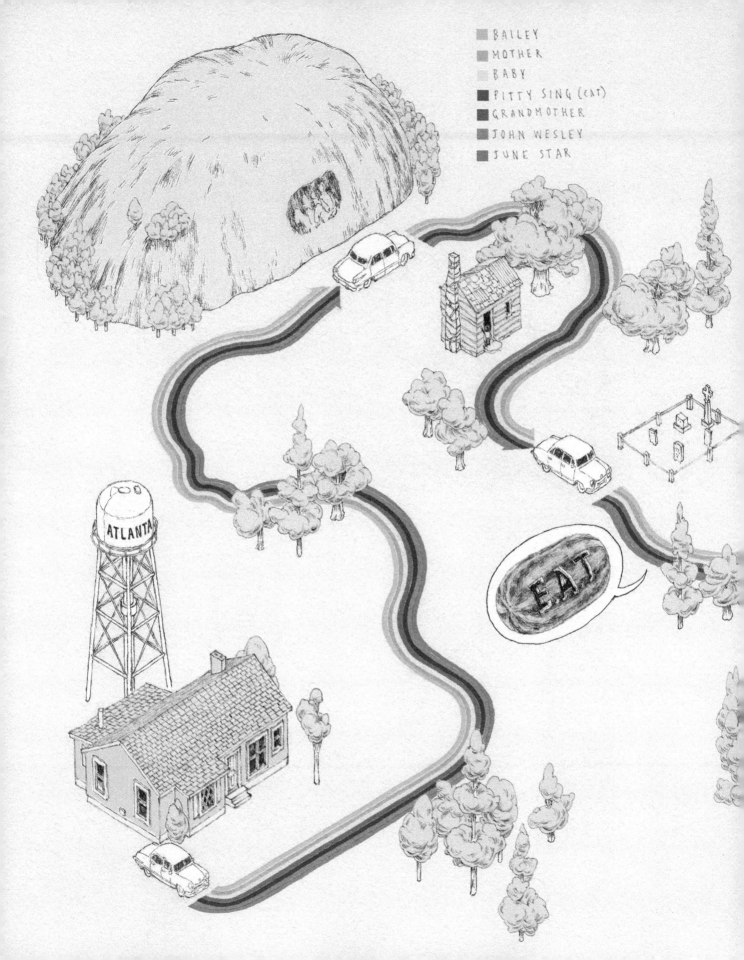

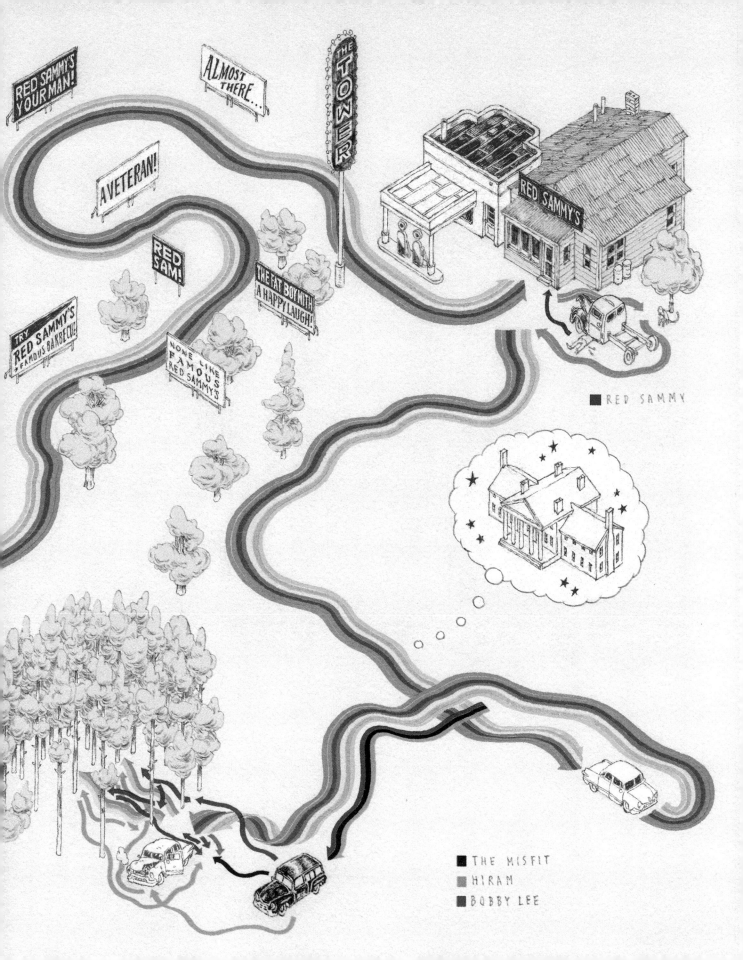

RED SAMMY'S YOUR MAN!

ALMOST THERE...

THE TOWER

A VETERAN!

RED SAM!

RED SAMMY'S

THE FAT BOY WITH A HAPPY LAUGH!

TRY RED SAMMY'S FAMOUS BARBECUE!

NONE LIKE FAMOUS RED SAMMY'S

■ RED SAMMY

■ THE MISFIT
■ HIRAM
■ BOBBY LEE

The Wrinkled
Time Continuum

From *A Wrinkle in Time*
By Madeleine L'Engle
1962

A *Wrinkle in Time* is unique in a lot of ways, but for science-fiction lovers it's hard not to find L'Engle's reliance on knowledge (rather than technology) especially charming. There are no phasers here, no spaceships, no thrusters; instead, what our young protagonists have is a tesseract — that is, a fairly abstract phenomenon that allows them to travel through space and time. L'Engle's lack of interest in gadgetry is important because its result is just one less veil over the things that really matter: mystery, romance, drama, and wonder.

The simplicity of the tesseract as a narrative device results not only in a lack of technological clutter (in the map, as in the book), but also in a coherent, if massive, universe. We can take in L'Engle's enormous spaces in a single glance. But that coherence does not result in a lack of awe. The magic is there despite L'Engle's focus on science. In a way, math *is* magic. Knowledge *is* what drives our heroes across the galaxy. But we may be getting ahead of ourselves.

As in any great adventure tale for younger readers, *A Wrinkle in Time* possesses both an intimate human drama and an epic cosmic war. Charles Wallace, Meg, and Calvin may start out in search of Mr. Murry, but it doesn't take long before that quest is wrapped up in the larger mission of defeating "IT" and "The Black Thing." Despite the looming presence of these antagonists, the focus is never far away from the family at its center. We care about their battle with these dark forces because we care about them, we want them to be together, we want them to love one another. In these respects, the story sounds almost absurdly maudlin, but of course it doesn't read that way. In fact, *A Wrinkle in Time* is actually quite dark (not to say stormy) and takes care to really reckon with disappointment, disillusionment, and death. IT has the frightening power to change people's natures and obscure the stars — a threat that finds ready analogues in the experience of childhood, a time when the world is porous and unstable. Even if the enemies are fictional, the threat here is recognizably real.

All this talk of darkness though does a disservice to L'Engle's equally fascinating consideration of love and light. In her world, the stars are our angels — a metaphor that seems central to the book. Angels are, of course, a traditionally religious conception, whereas stars are real, physical things. Stars are the subject of science, and for two millennia now we have been learning about them by using perhaps the most ancient human science there is: the art of Geometry. But then again, stars are beautiful, impossibly distant things. We wish on them as well. L'Engle's world is a deeply ordered world — but it's also a magical place. No wonder it remains so beloved. ●

MEG MURRY
CHARLES WALLACE MURRY
CALVIN O'KEEFE
MRS. WHATSIT
MRS. WHICH
MRS. WHO
MR. MURRY
MRS. MURRY
SANDY MURRY
DENNYS MURRY
AUNT BEAST

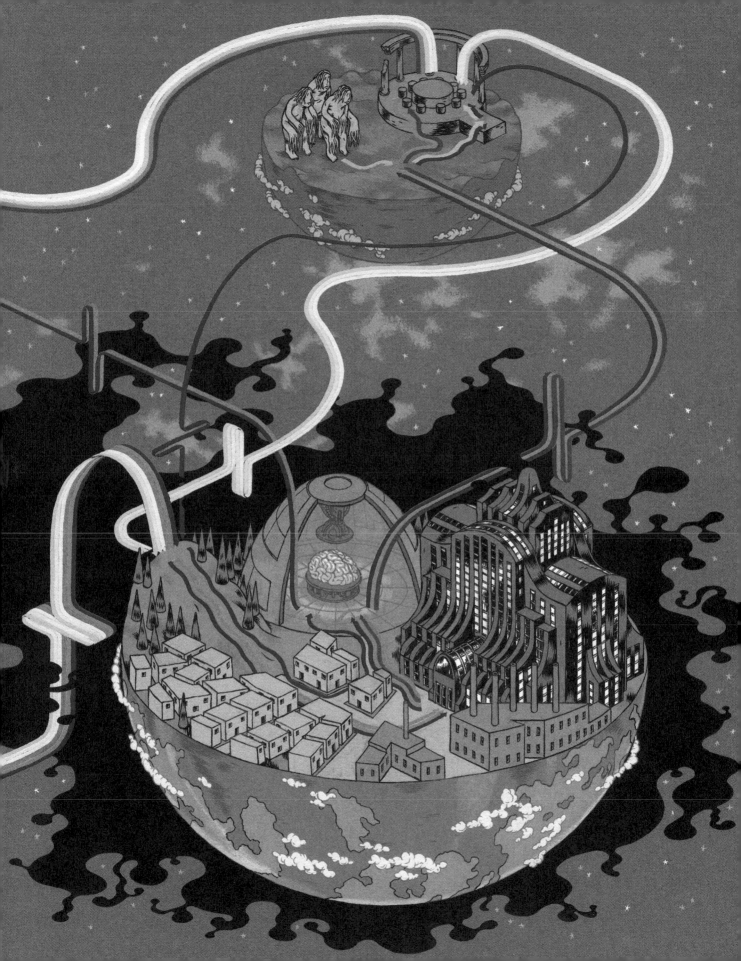

The Warrens

From *Watership Down*
By Richard Adams
1972

I t's commonly said of great books that they show us a new way of looking at the world. In Richard Adams's (incredibly adult) children's classic, that is literally the case. He took an area that he knew extremely well — the area that surrounded his home in the English country-side — and then made it home to an entirely new world, where rabbits talk and reason a lot like humans do but also remain, in a very real sense, rabbits. There is very little else like it in this regard. And perhaps that's the reason why so many publishers turned it down before it was finally released, won the Carnegie Medal, and sold millions upon millions of copies.

The humanish rabbits (or rabbity humans — whichever you prefer) of *Watership Down* show us a world that is both utterly recognizable and yet entirely new, with plants that smell more vivid, human symbols that seem more mysterious, and natural clues that offer far more information than we would normally expect. The essential nature of these rabbits — timid, yet capable of real bravery; limited in imagination, but creative when occasion demands; and generally imbued with the potential to exceed their natural limits — is the thing that binds us to them, and which makes their story matter. When Blackberry figures out how the rabbits can utilize a raft, Fiver gets it; but Hazel, who's a very clever rabbit in his own right, just cant grasp it. It's those little things that keep the rabbits in scale.

Scale was also an interesting problem to consider in creating these three maps. How to show how intimidatingly large the world beyond the Sandleford warren must appear, while at the same time offering an intimate glimpse of the rabbits' lives underground, of how they must feel under threat, as at Sandleford; defeated, as in Cowslip's warren; belligerent, as at Efrafa; or comfortable at a true home, as Watership Down finally becomes. On this question of scale, Richard Adams has, in a way, already provided the answer. We must see the rabbits as he understands them: on their own terms, but through a human lens. •

THIS IDEALLY SITUATED ESTATE
COMPRISING SIX ACRES OF EXCELLENT
BUILDING LAND, IS TO BE DEVELOPED
WITH HIGH CLASS MODERN RESIDENCES
BY
SUTCH & MARTIN LTD
OF NEWBURY, BERKS

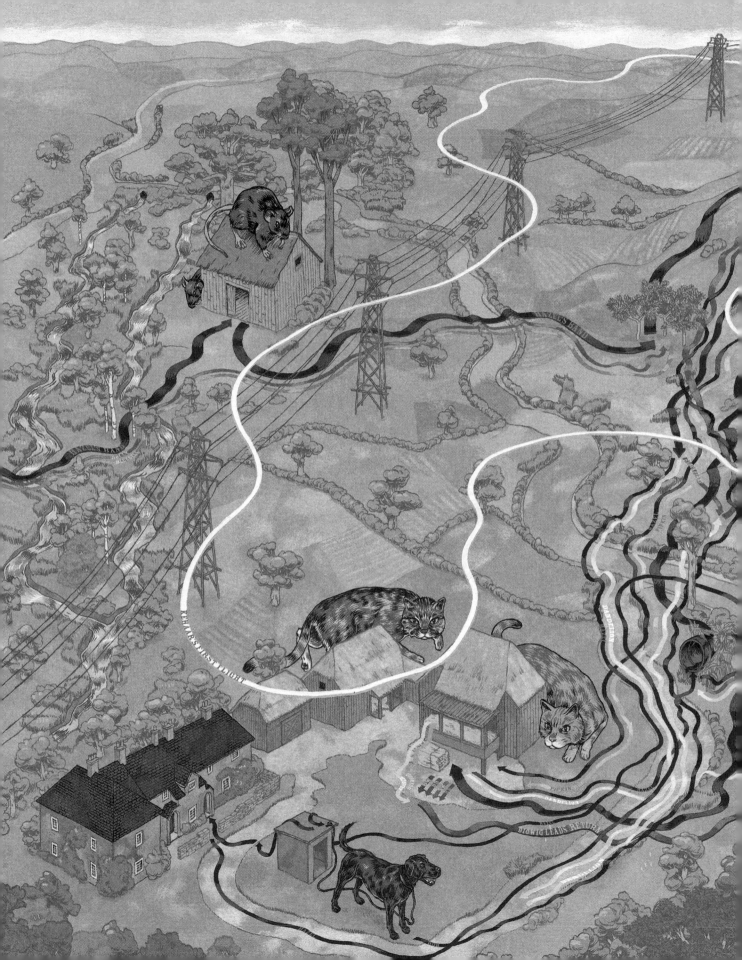

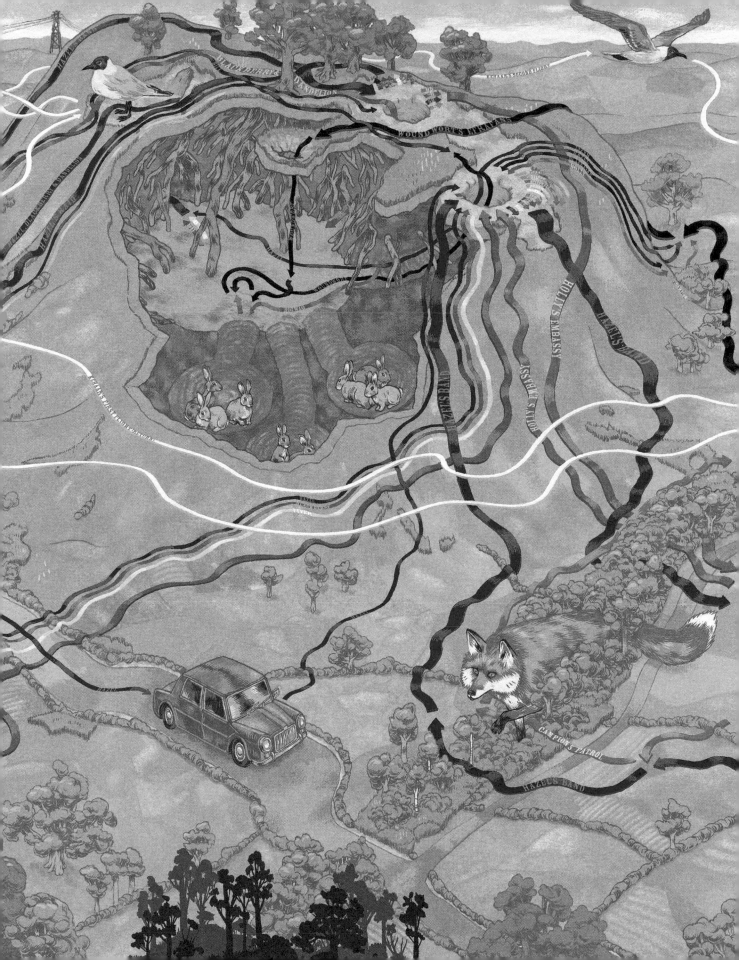

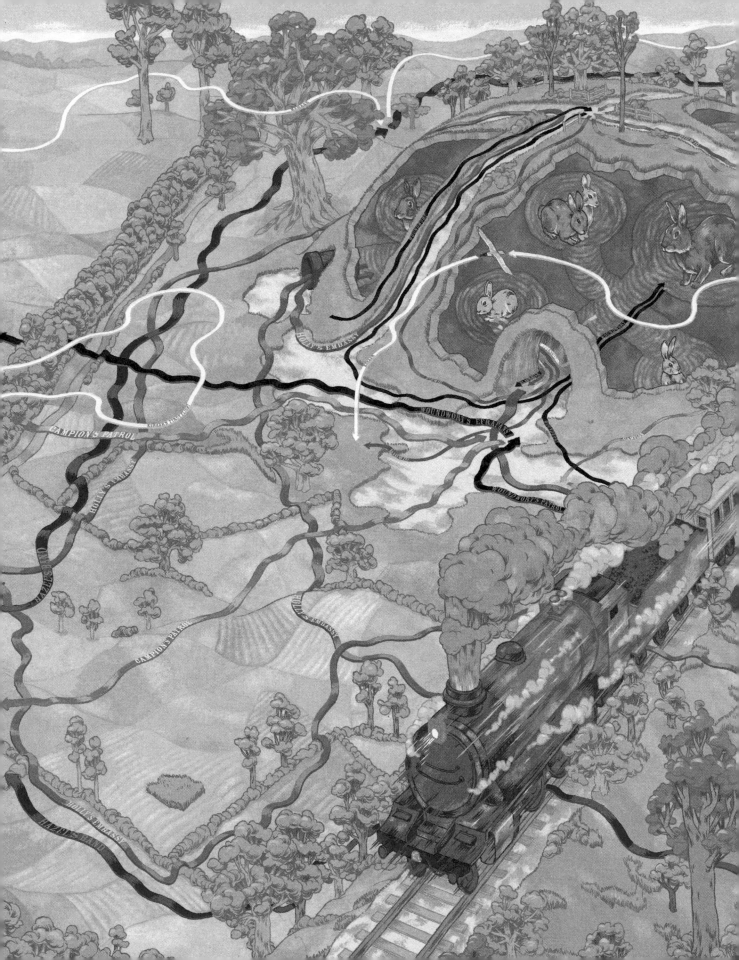

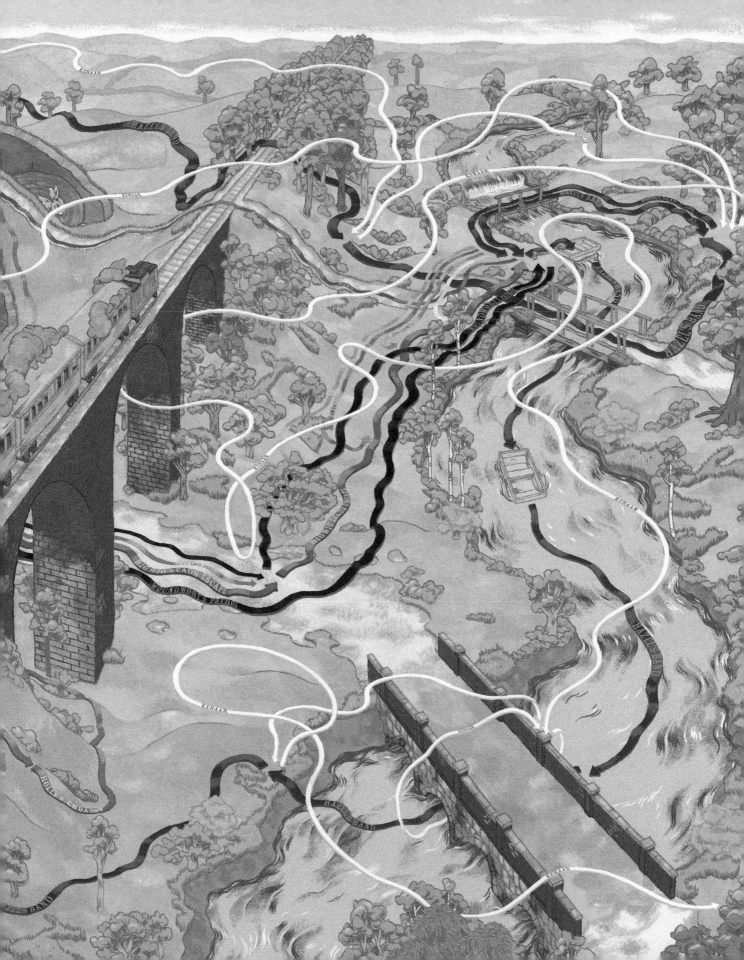

Those Who Leave and Those Who Stay

From "The Ones Who Walk Away from Omelas"
By Ursula K. Le Guin
1973

"The Ones Who Walk Away from Omelas" is not intended as a happy story. The city is built on human misery. It has a heart of darkness that everyone must witness. But even bearing all of that in mind, this is a civilization that still shines more brightly than any that we have ever seen. As opposed to being built on the bones of millions like the most vaunted nations of the present day, Omelas has a body count of one. That is an impressive record indeed. But the story's power seems to take advantage of that little cost. "One death is a tragedy," Stalin is supposed to have said, "one million is a statistic." One million is also truer to life but harder to see and compute. This single, unbearable life on display in Omelas forces us to reckon with our acquiescence in the brutal practices that remain a part of every civilization on earth.

This moral seems clear enough, but the story allows for a tremendous amount of complexity within its few pages. Ursula K. Le Guin won't make sense of the story's paradoxes for us. In fact, she forces us to partake of her creative act. She will not tell us about the technological sophistication of Omelas: "Perhaps it would be best if you imagined it as your own fancy bids... For certainly I cannot suit you all." Much in this city seems to be negotiable in this fashion; drugs and sex certainly are. But whatever else changes, the child prisoner must remain. Here we have no choice — but we can walk away. Which brings us back to this question of guilt.

"One thing I know there is none of in Omelas is guilt." This despite the fact that everyone within the city's walls is guilty to the same degree. Guilty as both participants in a horrible crime, and guilty of a self-willed ignorance. But do we live in this city, or are we the ones who walk away? The narrator herself seems to occupy an ambiguous place. Sometimes she seems to discuss the appearance of the city with the knowledge and familiarity of a local (even defending its practices at one point), but at other times she seems to drift away, gaining the perspective of a visitor rather than a resident. She seems to register what is strange about this place. But she cannot describe what lies beyond, in "the darkness" outside of Omelas, because each person there must make her own way. It is clearly an act of bravery to walk away, to stride into the unknown. As readers, Le Guin provides us with the building blocks to construct the city of Omelas, but if we want to forsake it afterward, then we too have to strike out alone. It is telling that it is "the ones" who walk away. It connotes a plurality of solitary units. That also sounds like a definition of civilization, but no one has yet returned to the city to tell of a civilization beyond those walls.

We only believe in Omelas, the perfect city, after misery is added to the description. And thus it remains a fair question: Can we believe in a city with that misery extracted? Can we even imagine such a thing? •

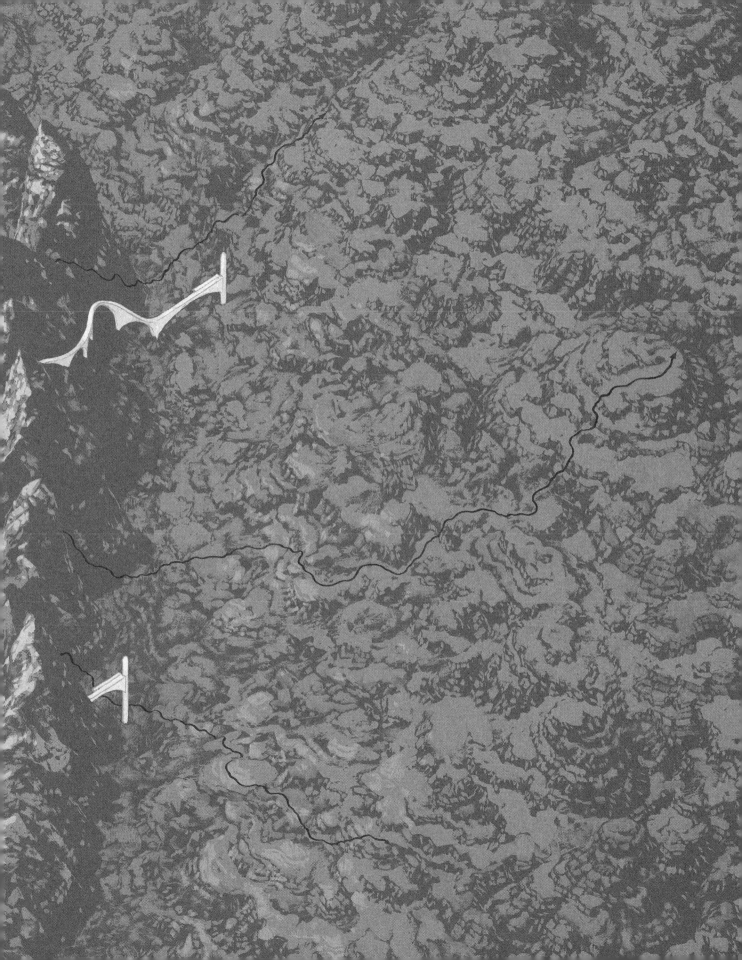

Further Reading

Barber, Peter. *The Map Book.* Walker & Company, 2005.

A rich collection of 175 gorgeous maps of different parts of the world from throughout human history, accompanied by short essays by map historians. Barber's book follows the progress of mapmaking from hand-drawn illustrations to digital renderings, and reads the history of man and the world through maps of our own making.

Brotton, Jerry. *A History of the World in 12 Maps.* Penguin Books, 2014.

A historical work considering how twelve maps (plus a number of additional cartographic works providing context) are intrinsically connected to the political views and campaigns of the times in which they were made.

Eco, Umberto. *The Book of Legendary Lands.* Rizzoli Ex Libris, 2013.

Eco's beautiful monograph provides an illustrated tour of great imaginary worlds found in literature, from Gulliver's Travels *to* The Lord of the Rings *to* Alice's Adventures in Wonderland. *The maps are paired with rich information and offer a unique perspective on how literature and reality inform one another.*

Garfield, Simon. *On the Map: A Mind-Expanding Exploration of the Way the World Looks.* Gotham, 2013.

What are maps to us, and why are we obsessed with them? Garfield takes a closer look at our relationships with worlds laid out before us on paper and delves into specific historical maps that speak to more than just location and distance.

Harmon, Katharine. *You Are Here: Personal Geographies and Other Maps of the Imagination.* Princeton Architectural Press, 2003.

Harmon explores the different constructions of maps and how they each express space, meaning, and time. Some examples include a "hand map," a "map of tenderness" drawn on the bottom of someone's feet, and a "map of the various paths of life."

Harmon, Katharine, and Gayle Clemans. *The Map as Art: Contemporary Artists Explore Cartography.* Princeton Architectural Press, 2010.

A follow-up to You Are Here, *Harmon extends her map collection and adds 360 new renderings by various artists, with their commentaries on how they construct and perceive their maps.*

Jennings, Ken. *Maphead: Charting the Wide, Weird World of Geography Wonks.* Scribner, 2012.

Best known for his record-breaking run on Jeopardy!, *Jennings takes us around the world to show us how maps are an integral part of how we see and interact with the world. Though* Maphead *actually has more text than maps, it's written in a wonderfully entertaining voice with funny anecdotes, clever insights, and a deep love and understanding for maps that will interest even those who don't like geography.*

Turchi, Peter. *Maps of the Imagination: The Writer as Cartographer.* Trinity University Press, 2007.

This is a book as much about writing as it is about maps. For the book and map lovers out there, Maps of the Imagination *examines the process of how we create landscape and geography from stories and narratives in our minds to physically realizing these worlds on paper.*

And don't forget about all the great books and stories that we've mapped here!

Acknowledgments

There are a lot of people to thank for helping making this book possible, but first among them is my wonderful wife, Michelle. This never would have happened without her encouragement and support. Helping with research, art direction, color-consultations — she's been utterly amazing. I would also like to thank my family, Mom and Dad in particular, for welcoming me as their "artist-in-residence" while we were in the middle of moving, and for their encouragement and excitement about the book throughout. They both instilled in me the importance of books and nurtured a joy in reading that I hope this book might now provide for others as well. (Thanks are also owed to them for art school. And for letting me draw in church — and everywhere else.) Over the past year my mom in particular has provided cheerleading, conversation breaks, and book recommendations, and has been the kind of one-woman PR machine that only one's mom can be. She is also an incredible teacher, and this book has a lot do with her. My brother and I are but two of the hundreds who have been lucky enough to call her their teacher, and I was fueled as much by her spirit as my own. Thanks to my brother, Nate, for listening to me complain, and doing so with friendship, humor, and compassion as you always have. And to Katie and Ellie (a.k.a. Baby Squishy) for starring in all of those amazing videos, which mean so much when you're across the country and missing your family — especially the rookies (that means you too, Baby V.).

Thanks to my invaluable intern and Philly summer studio mate, the talented Andrew Diemer. Thanks to the all the Communication Design faculty and students at Pratt Institute for advice and inspiration. Thanks to Gallery1988 for showing, promoting, and supporting my movie maps over the past seven years. And thanks to all the people who have bought a painting or print and supported this strange, wonderful project of mapping fiction.

Lastly, thanks to everyone at Zest Books for the faith in me and this project. Thanks to Olivia Ngai for all the timelines, synopses, internet-combing, and just generally amazing research. Thanks to this book's designer, Adam Grano, for putting it all together and making it all make sense (and look good at the same time). Finally, thanks to Daniel Harmon for finding my maps, creating this quest, and then sharing in the adventure as editor, co-conspirator, and consigliere. —AD

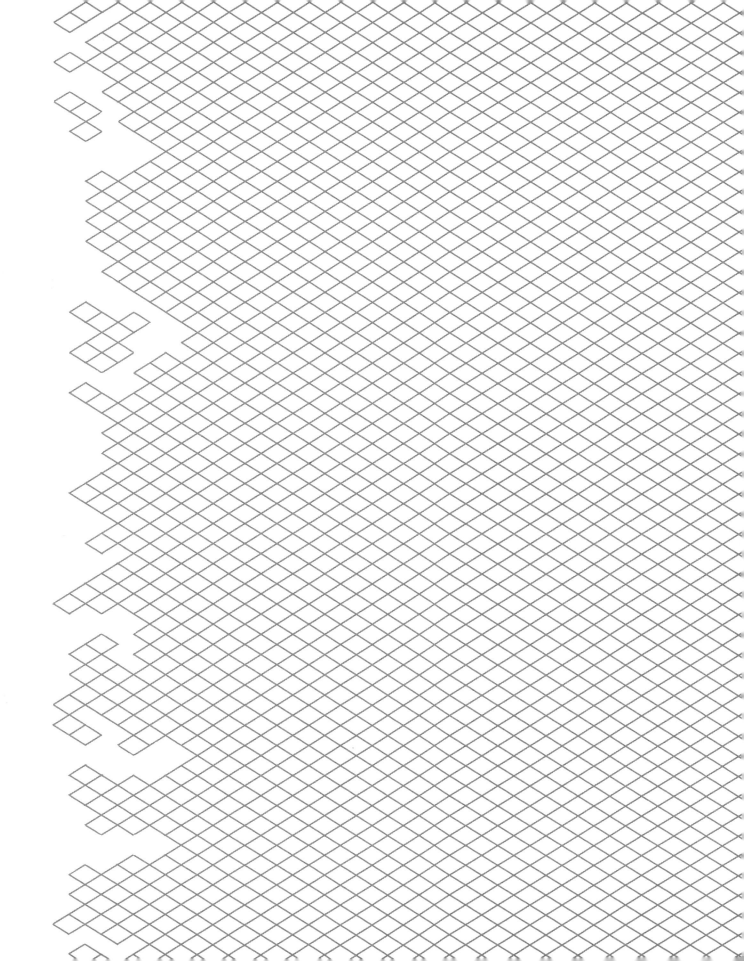

Andrew DeGraff *(left) is a freelance illustrator based in the San Francisco Bay Area. His clients include Kellogg's, Visa, Gap Kids, Bed Bath & Beyond, the* New York Times, *and the* New York Observer. *You can view more of his work at AndrewDegraff.com.*

Daniel Harmon *(right) is a former staff writer for Brokelyn.com, an occasional essayist on the topic of Tommy Wiseau's film* The Room, *and the author of the book* Super Pop! Pop Culture Top Ten Lists to Help You Win at Trivia, Survive in the Wild, and Make It Through the Holidays *(2013).*